MONTIGNAC

PROVENÇAL

COOK BOOK

MONTIGNAC PROVENÇAL COOK BOOK

MICHEL MONTIGNAC

By the same author:

Dine Out and Lose Weight

Eat Yourself Slim

The Montignac Method – Just for Women

Recipes and Menus

The Miracle of Wine

First Published 1997 by Montignac Publishing UK Ltd
1 Lumley Street LONDON W1Y 2NB

Text © Nutrimont/Montignac Publishing UK Ltd
Photographs © Montignac Publishing UK Ltd.

ISBN 2 90 623684 5

Food and location photography by Stuart Rothey
Food preparation and styling by Anneke Felderhof

Graphic design by Design / Section, Frome

Printed and bound in Great Britain by Butler & Tanner Ltd, Frome and London

Colour separations by Radstock Reproductions Ltd, Midsomer Norton

Jacket printed by Lawrence Allen Ltd, Weston-super-Mare

Publisher's Notes

The recipes in this book are based on metric measurements: the imperial measurements are only approximate.

Where olive oil is indicated in the recipes, extra virgin olive oil should be used whenever possible.

Goose fat can normally be obtained from a good butcher. Before long we hope it will also be available from supermarkets. However, should you experience difficulties obtaining supplies in your area, please contact us on 01277 218616.

The Montignac Food Range and other foods compatible with the Montignac Method are obtainable from:

Montignac Food Boutique & Café
160 Old Brompton Road LONDON SW5 0BA

Phone/fax 0171 370 2010
E-mail: ehilton@netcomuk.co.uk

Open from 8.30-7.30 daily except on Saturday 5.00.
Closed Sundays.

Fish   182

Shellfish   220

Side Dishes   230

Salads 262

Desserts 284

Menus for three months 322
(Weight Reduction Programme)

Foreword

One of the main aims of the two hundred recipes in this book, is that they should be simple, quick and practical – and as much as possible, use ingredients that are easily obtainable and not expensive.

These days, the time taken to perform a task like cooking appears to be a matter of considerable importance. Those that investigate these things tell us, that the time spent on producing the evening meal, is on average no more than twenty minutes. We are also told that many people have given up cooking for themselves or their family because they lack the time necessary to perform the task, and that they resort to the more expensive and less satisfying pastime of eating various forms of prepared food.

Hopefully, this book will allow these people to rediscover the pleasure of cooking, since none of these recipes need take more than thirty minutes to prepare – and most of them need take only twenty!

This book presupposes a basic knowledge of how to cook. It is after all, a recipe book and not a teaching manual. However, it is a recipe book with a difference. It is a recipe book written with the aim of reconciling apparent opposites.

For these days we live in a world of extremes. We have on the one hand people who seem determined to end their lives as soon as possible by indulging to excess in foods they know are bad for them. And on the other hand, we have people who appear to have almost sado-masochistic dietary attitudes that are prescriptive, symbolically frugal and obsessed with calorie counting.

The Montignac philosophy is an attempt to reconcile these opposites – showing it is possible to eat healthily and control your weight, yet still eat well and enjoy your food.

The Montignac philosophy is aimed at helping the western world return to good, sensible eating habits, where traditional cooking is married to the latest scientific discoveries about nutrition. In its application as a method for losing weight in a healthy and sustainable way, it is a challenge to the theories of an outdated dietary system of counting calories, where man is seen as an engine and not a complex, dynamic, living organism.

The Provençale Cookbook and the Montignac Method

All the recipes in this book are drawn from the culinary traditions of the Provence region of France and conform to the Montignac nutritional philosophy, which aims to help people develop a balanced and healthy diet without sacrificing the pleasures associated with eating good food. The recipes are easy to prepare, quick and economical. They are also high in nutrients to stimulate the metabolism, induce a healthy body and inhibit weight gain.

All the recipes are also compatible with the Montignac Method. This is a method for losing weight and maintaining that weight loss – based on recent studies into the human metabolism – which is quite different in character from traditional calorie-controlled diets that have plagued our lives for the last fifty years. Those interested in knowing more about the Montignac Method, will find a list of titles available in English at the front of this book.

All the recipes in this book are suitable for use in **Phase 1**, the weight-loss phase of the method, except those that belong to the weight-maintenance phase of the diet, which are marked **Phase 2**. There are also some recipes that happen to be suitable for vegetarians and these have been marked with a **V** for easy identification.

Those currently applying the Montignac weight-loss method will find it useful to refer to the section at the end of this book. Here I have compiled a three-month menu plan, which shows how the method can be implemented and may be used as a framework for individual plans.

Perhaps I should add at this point that none of the recipes in this book contain what I have termed elsewhere 'bad carbohydrates' – such as sugar, refined flour, potatoes, sweetcorn and certain types of rice – all of which give rise to high levels of sugar in the bloodstream. Some of these bad carbohydrates – particularly sugar and flour – feature prominently in many traditional sauces. So the sauces I use, are based only on thickening agents and flavourings compatible with my method.

This book also has several recipes designed to replace the eternal round of pasta, potatoes and rice dishes that figure far too prominently in our western diet. There are for instance, several recipes using alternative starchy foods like beans and lentils, which are far better for our metabolism. And since the rustic cuisine of Provence is famous for its distinctive vegetable dishes, many of these are to be found in this book as well.

Those familiar with the books I have written since 1986, will know that I have a strong attachment to the cuisine of the Provence. It is an attachment that has been re-enforced since coming to live in the south-east of France and particularly so from the day international health authorities came to recognise Mediterranean cuisine as the best in the world in terms of cardio-vascular disease prevention.

In this book, I have proposed certain culinary options that initially may cause some surprise if not the occasional growl or shrug of the shoulders – particularly if those traditional cooks happen to be French!

The first of these options is the total banning of butter as a cooking fat.

This of course, is in direct opposition to the recommendations of master chefs and cooks respected for their culinary expertise. Even in the classic dishes of the Provence, butter features in a large number of recipes.

This practice has its origins in the fact that butter used to be a rare and expensive product and therefore noble. Cooking with butter was a privilege of the rich and was thus incorporated into the dishes prepared for them by their cooks. As a consequence, the gastronomic traditions of the French are based on cooking with butter.

When you visit the kitchens of a famous French restaurant, seated in splendour near the cooking range, you will find a large pot of oily liquid preserved in a bain-marie – clarified butter. Purged of its impurities, it is then used to cook at temperatures beyond 120°C and to prepare a large number of sauces.

However, it is important to know that although butter is beneficial from a nutritional point of view if consumed melted or in its natural state in limited quantities of 10 to 25g per day (or no more than ¾oz), when cooked at temperatures in excess of 100°C this is no longer the case.

The fatty acids, which can be easily digested by enzymes in the small intestine, are completely destroyed around 100°C. When this happens, cooked butter becomes indigestible and difficult to break down: also it becomes harmful. Above 120°C, butter becomes completely denatured and turns black, producing a carcinogenic substance called acroleic.

When a nub of butter is put into the pan to cook a traditional recipe, the temperature of the fat will normally reach 160 or 180°C, at which point it is potentially harmful to the person for whom the dish is being prepared.

This is why I recommend using goose fat (though duck fat or olive oil may be used if goose fat is difficult to obtain) for all recipes that exceed 100°C (212°F) during the cooking process.

Goose fat is a good cooking fat for three main reasons.

First of all it is principally a mono-unsaturated fat. It is therefore very similar in its chemical structure and behaviour to olive oil, which almost everyone acknowledges these days, is extremely good for your health.

Secondly, goose fat has one particular advantage over all other fats – it can support temperatures in excess of 200°C (392°F) and still keep its molecular structure intact. As a result, even after it has been cooked, it still remains digestible and beneficial to the cardio-vascular system.

Finally, it imparts the most delicious flavour to the food cooked in it. It is therefore quite indispensable to anyone serious about good food, whether or not they are concerned about their health

Many recipes suggest using Soya Cream instead of Crème Fraîche.

This is a relatively new ingredient that became available in France in 1995. Initial reactions to its use in the kitchen seem to be favourable, in that it enables the cook to produce a creamy sauce without using saturated fats like Crème Fraîche or Whipping Cream. In my view, it is particularly suited for use in sauces to accompany fish and vegetables. However, if used to accompany meat, I would suggest lifting the flavour of the sauce by adding a little goose fat.

The only problem I have encountered cooking with this ingredient, is that it will curdle if cooked over a high heat or for too long. It is therefore not suitable for dishes that need to simmer for any length of time. However, if added at the end of the cooking process or as a deglazing medium, it is ideal.

Another option I propose in this book, is cooking at low temperature.

Whether we are cooking onions in a pan, or vegetables, fish, crustacea or even some meats like chicken, there is absolutely no need to use high temperature that will caramelise or burn the food.

This process is known as the Maillard effect, because this scientist was the first to demonstrate that the application of heat will cause a breakdown in the molecular structure of food. For instance, the brown pigments and polymers that appear when food is subjected to high temperatures, are the by-products of the denaturation of proteins and sugars. According to people like P. Dang (1990), the new substances produced as a result of this type of cooking, are both toxic and carcinogenic.

When you have problems digesting a meal – perhaps when you have been to a restaurant and one with a good reputation – your problems are probably attributable to the excessive temperatures applied when cooking your food. What effects these factors may have on your health in the long term, it is impossible to say at this stage.

Finally, in connection with general cooking practice, I would recommend that oil used in cooking should be discarded and replaced with fresh oil before serving. This will make your food easier to digest and your health will benefit.

Suggested Combinations of
SPICES AND

Beef: Garlic, Basil, Cumin, Curry, Ginger, Bay, Marjoram, Oregano, Pimiento, Cayenne pepper, Thyme

Chicken: Garlic, Basil, Bay, Coriander, Chives, Curry, Ginger, Marjoram, Oregano, Tarragon, Thyme

Lamb: Garlic, Basil, Cumin, Mint, Oregano, Rosemary, Thyme

Pork: Garlic, Dill, Coriander, Curry, Cumin, Ginger, Cayenne pepper, Rosemary, Sage, Thyme

Veal: Garlic, Dill, Coriander, Bay, Oregano, Rosemary, Sage, Thyme

Eggs: Chives, Cumin, Curry, Tarragon, Cayenne pepper, Savoury

Fish: Dill, Chives, Coriander, Tarragon, Bay, Nutmeg, Sage, Thyme

Seafood: Dill, Basil, Chervil, Cloves, Coriander, Curry, Tarragon, Bay, Marjoram, Oregano, Thyme

Rice: Garlic, Chives, Cumin, Curry, Tarragon, Sage

HERBS

Asparagus: Dill, Basil, Chives, Tarragon, Sesame seeds, Nutmeg

Aubergines: Garlic, Basil, Marjoram, Oregano, Pimiento, Sage, Thyme

Broad Bean: Dill, Basil, Chives, Tarragon, Marjoram, Savoury, Sage, Oregano, Rosemary

Broccoli: Garlic, Basil, Cumin, Curry, Ginger, Marjoram, Oregano, Tarragon, Thyme

Brussel Sprouts: Garlic, Basil, Cumin, Curry, Ginger, Marjoram, Oregano, Tarragon, Thyme

Cabbage: Garlic, Basil, Cumin, Curry, Ginger, Marjoram, Oregano, Tarragon, Thyme

Cauliflower: Garlic, Basil, Cumin, Curry, Ginger, Marjoram, Oregano, Tarragon, Thyme

Courgettes: Garlic, Dill, Basil, Chives, Tarragon, Marjoram, Mint, Oregano

Dried Bean: Garlic, Coriander, Cumin, Tarragon, Marjoram, Oregano, Pimiento, Cayenne pepper, Rosemary, Savoury, Sage, Thyme

French Bean: Garlic, Dill, Basil, Tarragon, Bay, Marjoram, Mint, Rosemary, Savoury

Mushrooms: Garlic, Dill, Basil, Chives, Tarragon, Marjoram, Oregano, Rosemary

Peas: Dill, Basil, Chive, Tarragon, Marjoram, Mint, Oregano, Savoury

Peppers: Garlic, Chives, Coriander, Tarragon, Marjoram, Oregano, Thyme

Spinach: Garlic, Basil, Tarragon, Nutmeg

Tomatoes: Garlic, Dill, Chives, Coriander, Tarragon, Marjoram, Oregano, Rosemary, Savoury, Sage, Thyme

COCKTAILS

SNACKS

AND DIPS

Cocktail Snacks and Dips

One of the fundamental recommendations of the Montignac Method is that alcohol should never be drunk on an empty stomach.

The Golden Rule is that first you should eat and then drink.

Here then are a few suggestions how to satisfy what should be a responsibility, even for those who have no weight problem.

Snacks for those on Phase 1

- slices of cured sausage
- salami
- chorizos
- rolled cooked ham
- rolled cured ham
- rolled smoked salmon
- green olives
- black olives
- cheese cubes
- raw vegetables (carrots, cauliflower sprigs, celery sticks, chicory leaves) Ⓥ
- radishes, tomatoes, cherries Ⓥ

Snacks for those on Phase 2

- canapé from pain intégrale (bread made from unrefined flour), with foie gras, smoked salmon, caviar or potted goose
- crab sticks
- bacon rolled on asparagus sticks

Beurre de Céleri au Roquefort
Celery and Roquefort Butter

Preparation : 5 minutes
No cooking

Phase 2

- 150g (5oz) Roquefort cheese
- 50g (2oz) soft butter
- 1 large celery stick
- 4 tablespoons fat reduced (15%) crème fraîche
- 3 teaspoons armagnac
- salt, freshly ground pepper

Wash the stick of celery. Remove the leaves and threads. Cut into lengths.

Purée the celery, butter, Roquefort, crème fraîche and armagnac in a blender. Season to taste.

Spread the mixture on chicory leaves or prepared raw vegetables.

Arrange on a serving dish.

Sauce Cocktail au Roquefort
Cocktail Sauce with Roquefort

Preparation : 5 minutes
No cooking

- 100g (4oz) Roquefort cheese
- 2 small natural yoghurts
- 2 tablespoons chopped parsley
- freshly ground pepper

Crumble the roquefort with a fork.

In a bowl, mix the cheese with the yoghurt to obtain a rich cream.

Add the chopped parsley and pepper.

Serve in a bowl.

Mousse de Concombre au Chèvre Frais
Cucumber Mousse with Fresh Goats Cheese

Preparation : 10 minutes
No cooking

- 250g (9oz) chèvre cheese – well drained
- 1 cucumber
- 2 tablespoons olive oil
- 1 tablespoon strong mustard
- 3 tablespoons chopped chives
- salt, freshly ground pepper

Peel the cucumber. Slice in two lengthways. Remove the seeds and dice the flesh. Leave to drain for 30 minutes.

Purée the chèvre cheese, cucumber, olive oil and mustard in a blender. Fold in the chopped chives and season to taste.

Chill and keep in the fridge until required.

Note: If following Phase 1, exclude mustard from the recipe.

Top, Ham Mousse
with avocado

Middle, Cucumber
Mousse with fresh
goats cheese

Bottom, Paprika and
cheese cocktail sauce

Mousse de Jambon à l'Avocat
Ham Mousse with Avocado

Preparation : 5 minutes
No cooking

Phase 2

- 150g (5oz) cooked ham with fat removed
- 50g (2oz) cured ham with fat removed
- 2 ripe avocados
- 1 tablespoon olive oil
- 3 tablespoons crème fraîche
- 1 tablespoon cognac
- juice of ½ lemon
- salt, freshly ground pepper and tabasco

Cut the avocados in two and remove the flesh.

Put the avocado, chopped ham, olive oil, lemon juice, cognac, crème fraîche, dash of tabasco, salt and pepper in the mixer and beat until creamy.

Serve chilled.

Sauce Cocktail au Paprika et au Fromage Ⓥ
Paprika and Cheese Cocktail Sauce

Preparation : 5 minutes
No cooking

- 400g (14oz) fromage frais
- 2 cloves garlic – puréed
- 1 bunch parsley
- 1 bunch chervil
- 1 bunch dill
- 20 black olives – stoned
- ½ teaspoon paprika
- 1 tablespoon olive oil
- salt, freshly ground pepper

Drain the fromage frais through a cheesecloth. Purée in a blender with the crushed garlic, chopped parsley, chives, dill, chopped black olives, paprika and olive oil. Season to taste.

Place in the fridge for at least 2 hours.

Serve as a sauce to be eaten with raw vegetables.

Sauce Cocktail à la Tomate
Tomato Cocktail Sauce

Preparation : 5 minutes
No cooking

- 3 small full milk yoghurts
- 3 tablespoons tomato purée
- 1 clove garlic – crushed
- 1 tablespoon olive oil
- 2 teaspoons thyme
- salt, freshly ground pepper, cayenne

In a bowl combine the yoghurts, tomato purée and olive oil to make a uniform, creamy mixture.

Add the garlic and thyme. Stir well.

Season with salt, pepper and cayenne. Store in the fridge for 2 or 3 hours before serving.

Mousse de Thon
Tuna Mousse

Preparation : 10 minutes
No cooking

- 250g (9oz) tuna in brine
- 1 small tin of anchovies in olive oil
- 150g (5oz) green olives – stoned
- 4 tablespoons olive oil
- 3 cloves garlic – crushed
- 3 teaspoons balsamic vinegar
- 3 teaspoons strong mustard
- 1 tablespoons crème fraîche
- freshly ground pepper

Drain the tuna and break down with a fork.

Put the tuna, anchovies and their oil, green olives, garlic, vinegar, mustard and crème fraîche in the blender.

Add pepper and blend until the mixture is smooth. Adjust the seasoning.

Serve chilled.

STARTERS

Marinade d'Aubergines
Aubergine Marinade

This dish may be eaten on its own or with other hors-d'œuvre.

Preparation : 5 minutes
   Cooking : 20 minutes

- 4 aubergines
- 2 cloves garlic
- 15cl (5fl oz) olive oil
- Herbes de Provence
- salt, freshly ground pepper, cayenne pepper

Cut the aubergines into round slices at least 1cm (½in) thick.

Cook in a steamer for 20 minutes and allow to drain.

Make a marinade in a bowl with the olive oil, crushed garlic, salt, freshly ground pepper and cayenne pepper.

In a stoneware dish, layer the slices of aubergine, brushing each layer with the marinade and dusting liberally with Herbes de Provence.

Make certain the layers of aubergine are pressed down well before covering the dish with plastic film and placing it in the fridge, where it can be kept for several days.

Aumônière à la Mousse de Saumon Fumé
Aumônière with Smoked Salmon Mousse

Line a teacup or ramekin with a generous slice of salmon and fill with the mousse. The edges of the salmon are then tied together with a strand of chive to make an Aumônière or pouch.

Serves 4
Preparation : 20 minutes
No cooking

- 16 Slices smoked salmon
- 200g (7oz) crème fraîche
- 20cl (7fl oz) whipping cream
- 1 tablespoon chopped dill
- 1 tablespoon chopped chives
- chive stalks
- parsley sprigs
- pepper

Reserve the 8 most attractive slices of smoked salmon to make the pouches.

Place the rest of the smoked salmon in a blender to make the purée.

Whip the cream in a large bowl after adding a pinch of salt.

Fold the whipped cream into the salmon purée, adding at the same time, half the dill and half the chopped chives.

Add pepper to taste.

Make the pouches using a teacup or ramekin, fill with the mousse and secure with two or three whole chive stalks.

Serve on a plate, decorate with the remaining herbs, parsley sprigs and salmon mousse.

Bavarois d'Avocat
Avocado Bavarois

Serves 5
Preparation : 15 minutes
No cooking

- 4 ripe avocados
- the juice of 1½ lemons
- 300g (10oz) fromage frais – strained
- 50g (2oz) stoned black olives
- 1½ tablespoon chopped fresh parsley
- 1 tablespoon chopped dill
- 1 tablespoon olive oil
- salt, freshly ground pepper, ground coriander
- cayenne pepper – 1 or 2 pinches

Mix the flesh of the avocados in a blender with the lemon juice, parsley, dill, black olives, salt, pepper, coriander and cayenne pepper.

Transfer to a bowl and mix together with the fromage frais that has been well strained. Adjust the seasoning to taste.

Pour the mixture into a mould or individual pastry rings and leave to set in the refrigerator for 4 to 5 hours.

Unmould and serve on a bed of lettuce. Decorate with parsley and some olives.

Pâté d'Avocat aux Crevettes
Avocado Pâté with Prawns

Serves 4   Phase 2
Preparation : 15 minutes
     Cooking : 2 minutes

- 5 ripe avocados
- 250g (9oz) prawns – peeled
- 2 lemons
- 12g (½oz) agar-agar
- 3 tablespoons Montbazillac
  (white semi-sweet wine from the Bergerac)
- 1 teaspoon ground green peppercorns
- salt, cayenne pepper

Pat the prawns dry.

Mix the avocado flesh with the lemon juice and the ground green peppercorns.

Dissolve the agar-agar in the Montbazillac by warming gently.

Season with salt and cayenne pepper and mix well.

Pour into a mould and pat down well.

Place in the fridge for at least 6 hours.

Serve on a bed of lettuce with a light mayonnaise.

Carpaccio de Boeuf
Beef Carpaccio

Carpaccio is prepared from raw beef, either top-rump or fillet, which has been finely sliced on a butcher's slicing machine. Ask your butcher to interleave with greaseproof paper to prevent the slices sticking together.
If preparing the meat at home, to make it firm and easier to handle freeze briefly before slicing.

Serves 4
Preparation : 10 minutes
No cooking

- 300g (10oz) Carpaccio
- olive oil
- granular sea salt
- freshly ground pepper
- Herbes de Provence

Arrange the Carpaccio on large plates.

Brush with olive oil.

Sprinkle lightly with the Herbes de Provence, coarse sea salt and pepper from the pepper mill.

Allow to stand and marinate for 10 to 15 minutes before serving.

Variation: Replace Herbes de Provence with flakes of Parmesan cheese thinly pared with a potato peeler.

Paillasson d'Oignons Gratinés
Cheese and Onion Rösti with Bacon

Serves 4
Preparation : 15 minutes
    Cooking : 20 minutes

- 8 onions
- 400g (14oz) grated Gruyère cheese
- 8 slices bacon
- olive oil
- freshly ground pepper

Peel and chop the onions.

Take a large pan, add olive oil and the chopped onions and heat gently to a golden brown. Season with freshly ground pepper.

Degrease the onion by turning out onto absorbent kitchen paper.

On individual oven-proof dishes make beds of onion and cover each portion with 100g (3½oz) of Gruyère cheese.

Cover each bed with 2 slices of bacon and place 10cm (4in) below the grill in a very hot oven, preheated to Mk.10 – 250°C.

Take out and serve when the cheese is lightly browned.

Soufflé au Fromage
Cheese Soufflé

Serves 4
Preparation : 25 minutes
   Cooking : 20 minutes

- 6 eggs
- 200g (7oz) grated cheese
- 4 tablespoons crème fraîche

Separate the yolks from the whites into two large bowls.

Mix the yolks and the grated cheese into a smooth cream. Season with salt and pepper to taste.

Lightly beat the crème fraîche and stir into the egg and cheese mixture.

Add a pinch of salt to the egg whites and beat until stiff. Fold delicately into the egg and cream mixture using a spatula.

Pour into an oiled soufflé dish.

Place into a preheated oven (Mk.5 – 190°C).

Raise the temperature of the oven (Mk.10 – 250°C) to ensure the soufflé rises and turns golden brown.

If you have a window in your oven, monitor the progress of the soufflé. Do not open the oven door until the soufflé reaches its optimum consistency and colour after about 20 minutes.

Serve immediately. A hot soufflé should never be kept waiting!

Terrine de Foies de Volaille
Chicken Liver Terrine

Serves 5/6
Preparation : 30 minutes
    Cooking : 1 hr 5 minutes

- 600g (1¼lb) chicken livers
- 3 chopped onions
- 4 cloves crushed garlic
- 500g (18oz) button mushrooms
- 20cl (7fl oz) whipping cream
- 5 egg yolks
- olive oil
- goose fat
- Herbes de Provence
- salt, freshly ground pepper, cayenne pepper

Trim the livers and brown in a non-stick pan cooking gently for a few minutes in goose fat. Season with salt, pepper, cayenne and Herbes de Provence. Reserve.

Clean and chop the mushrooms. Heat olive oil in the pan, brown and sweat the mushrooms over a gentle heat. Pour off the water that is released during cooking.

At the same time, in another pan heat olive oil and brown the chopped onions over a gentle heat.

Place the livers, mushrooms and onions (without their cooking juices) in a large bowl. Add the garlic, whipping cream and egg yolks. Season with salt, freshly ground pepper and cayenne. Put into a blender and reduce to a fine pulp.

Pour into an ovenware dish and dust with Herbes de Provence.

Put into a warm oven (Mk.3 – 160°C) for 45 minutes.

Serve in slices on a bed of lettuce, adding some gherkins.

Terrine de Foies de Volaille aux Poireaux
Chicken Liver and Leek Terrine

Serves 4/5
Preparation : 30 minutes
   Cooking : 50 minutes

- 10 leek whites
- 600g (1¼lb) chicken livers
- 4 chopped shallots
- 1 sachet gelatine powder
- ½ glass of sherry
- goose fat
- 75cl (3fl oz) chicken stock
- olive oil
- salt, freshly ground pepper, cayenne pepper

Cook the leek whites in the chicken stock for 30 minutes. Strain and reserve the leeks. Reserve the stock.

In a pan containing 1 tablespoon of goose fat, sauté the chicken livers and chopped shallots over a gentle heat. Season with salt, ground pepper and cayenne. Deglaze gently using the sherry vinegar.

Line the bottom of the earthenware terrine with leek whites.

Fill the terrine with alternate layers of chicken livers and the remaining leeks.

Dissolve the gelatine in 20cl (7fl oz) of the remaining stock.

Cover the terrine with the lukewarm jelly before it begins to set. Press down well and place in the fridge for 5 or 6 hours.

Turn out of the terrine and cut into slices 1.5cm (½in) thick.

Serve on a bed of lettuce.

Flan de Courgettes et de Poivrons
Courgette and Sweet Pepper Flan

Serves 6
Preparation : 25 minutes
    Cooking : 1 hr 5 minutes

- 1 kg (2¼lb) courgettes
- 4 red peppers
- 400g (14oz) fromage frais – strained
- 5 eggs
- 50g (2oz) grated Gruyère cheese
- 10cl (3½oz) double cream
- nutmeg
- Herbes de Provence
- salt, freshly ground pepper, olive oil

Cut the courgettes in three down their length. Cook in a steamer for 20 minutes. Reserve and drain, pressing gently to extract as much liquid as possible.

Cut the sweet peppers into halves. Remove the pith and the seeds. Place the peppers, skin side up, under the grill in the oven until the skin bubbles and is slightly charred. This will make removal of the skin much easier and improve the flavour of the peppers. Peel and cut into large strips.

In a bowl, beat the eggs and then blend with the strained fromage frais, nutmeg, Herbes de Provence and whipping cream. Salt and pepper to taste.

On the bottom of a cake tin coated with olive oil, spread out the vegetables, cover with the mixture and sprinkle with the grated Gruyère cheese.

Cook for 45 minutes in a very cool oven (Mk. ½ – 130° C).

Allow to cool completely and then place in the fridge for 6 hours.

Remove from the tin, cut into slices and dribble fresh olive oil over the top. Serve on a bed of lettuce.

Terrine de Feta à la Crétoise
Cretan Style Feta Terrine

Serves 6
Preparation : 30 minutes
    Cooking : 15 minutes

- 500g (1lb) genuine Greek Feta cheese
- 3 red peppers
- 3 cloves crushed garlic
- 3 tablespoons freshly chopped basil, together with 20 or so whole leaves
- 2 leaves gelatine (or some agar-agar)
- 20cl (7fl oz) olive oil
- 10cl (3½fl oz) full-fat crème fraîche
- 10 stoned, finely sliced black olives
- 1 tablespoon balsamic vinegar
- salt, freshly ground pepper
- fresh thyme
- bunch of parsley

Slice the peppers in half. Remove the pith and the seeds. Place under the grill skin side up until the skin bubbles and chars. Remove the skin and cut the peppers into strips 1cm (½in) wide.

Put the Feta cheese into a bowl and crush with the back of a spoon, mixing thoroughly with the olive oil at the same time. Add salt to taste. Add freshly ground pepper liberally.

Soften the gelatine leaves in cold water. Gently heat the crème fraîche (without bringing to the boil). Squeeze the gelatine to remove excess water, add to the warm pan and dissolve, stirring gently. Incorporate the Feta cheese.

Put the crushed garlic cloves, balsamic vinegar, freshly chopped basil, fresh thyme, sliced olives into a bowl and mix into a smooth paste.

Line a suitable cake tin with plastic film, adding alternate layers of cheese and peppers. Include two layers of basil leaves as the layers are built up to fill the tin.

Place in a fridge for at least 6 hours.

Cut into slices and serve on individual plates decorated with basil and parsley leaves.

Sardines Fraîches au Vinaigre de Xérès
Fresh Sardines with Sherry Vinegar

Serves 4
Preparation : 30 minutes
No cooking

- 1kg (2¼lb) fresh sardines
- 4 crushed shallots
- 4 or 5 bay leaves
- 1 glass sherry vinegar
- olive oil
- coarse sea salt, freshly ground pepper

Prepare the sardines: scale and gut under running water and remove the heads.

Remove the fillets by pulling along the backbone. Rinse and place in a shallow dish.

Mix the vinegar with the crushed shallots and cover the sardines. Lay the bay leaves flat on the sardines. Sprinkle 1 heaped tablespoon of coarse sea salt over the top.

Allow to marinate for 4 hours.

Then rinse the sardine fillets under the tap and lay them out to dry on absorbent kitchen paper.

Arrange the fillets in a shallow dish, sprinkle with olive oil and season liberally with freshly ground pepper. Decorate with lemon slices and serve.

Chèvres Marinés aux Fèves Fraîches
Marinated Goats Cheese with Fresh Broad Beans

Serves 4
Preparation : 20 minutes
Cooking : 2 minutes

- 4 small goat's cheeses or 4 slices, weighing about 300g (10oz) in all
- 10cl (4fl oz) olive oil
- 500g (1lb) fresh broad beans
- 4 teaspoons balsamic vinegar
- 1 teaspoon Herbes de Provence
- 1 clove garlic – crushed
- salt, pepper freshly ground, cayenne pepper

Halve or quarter the four portions of cheese. Place them in a deep dish and sprinkle with the Herbes de Provence.

Mix the olive oil and crushed garlic in a bowl, lightly dusting with cayenne pepper and freshly ground pepper.

Pour the marinade over the cheese, cover with plastic film and allow to marinate for a few hours.

Shell the beans. Plunge them into boiling salted water for 2 minutes and then remove the fine skin covering them.

Place the pieces of cheese on the plates, together with the beans.

Coat with a vinaigrette made from 4 tablespoons of the marinade mixed with the balsamic vinegar. Then serve.

Terrine de Lotte
Monkfish Terrine

Serves 6   Phase 2
Preparation : 25 minutes
    Cooking : 60 minutes

- 1.5kg (3¼lb) skinned and filleted monkfish
- 8 eggs
- 10cl (3½fl oz) double cream
- 2 tablespoons tomato purée
- 1 tablespoon finely chopped tarragon
- 5cl (2fl oz) brandy
- Court-bouillon
- 1 lemon
- salt, freshly ground pepper, cayenne
- home made mayonnaise
- 1 teaspoon tomato purée

Poach the monkfish for 12 minutes in the court-bouillon with the lemon juice.

Lift out of the pan and dry well on a tea towel. Cut the fillets into rectangular pieces.

Beat the eggs with the tomato concentrate and the double cream. Add salt, freshly ground pepper, cayenne pepper, tarragon and the brandy.

Place the monkfish in a lightly buttered tin and cover with the egg mixture.

Place the tin in a bain-marie before putting into a preheated oven (Mk.3 – 160°C) for 45 minutes. See whether the fish is cooked by testing with the point of a knife.

Allow to get cold before placing in the fridge for at least 5 or 6 hours.

When required, turn out of mould and cut into slices. Serve on individual plates on a bed of lettuce and decorate with home made mayonnaise, mixed with 1 teaspoon tomato purée.

Mousse de Fromage à la Provençale
Provençale Cheese Mousse

Serves 4
Preparation : 25 minutes
No cooking

- 400g (14oz) fromage frais – strained
- 1 large cucumber
- 2 egg whites
- 2 tablespoons chopped chives
- 2 tablespoons chopped parsley
- 2 tablespoons olive oil
- 2 cloves garlic – crushed
- 2 teaspoons strong mustard

Prepare 4 flan rings about 8cm (3in) in diameter.

Cut the cucumber into thin slices. Salt and drain.

Whisk the egg whites until stiff.

In a bowl, mix the strained fromage frais with the whisked egg whites, chopped parsley and chives, the olive oil, mustard and crushed garlic cloves. Salt and pepper to taste.

Place the rings on individual plates. Line the bottom and sides of the rings with the cucumber slices. Fill with the mixture. Cover with the remaining cucumber slices and place in the fridge for 3 hours.

Remove the rings and decorate with parsley or lettuce and dribble with olive oil before serving.

Noix de Saint-Jacques Marinées à l'Aneth
Scallops Marinated with Dill

Serves 4
Preparation : 15 minutes
No cooking

- 4 to 6 scallops per person
- fine sea salt
- 1 bunch dill
- freshly ground pepper
- olive oil

Put the scallops on a plate so that they do not touch each other and place in the freezer for 15 to 20 minutes so that they become firm without freezing solid.

Take a very sharp knife and finely slice the scallops.

Cover each plate with the scallop slices so they partially overlap each other like the scales of a fish.

Sprinkle with sea salt and pepper. Dribble with olive oil, spreading lightly all over the sliced scallops with a brush.

Sprinkle with finely chopped dill.

Cover with plastic film and allow at least 30 minutes to go by before serving.

Timbales de Saint-Jacques
Scallop Timbales

The timbales may be kept in the fridge and reheated at the last moment in a microwave or in a very cool oven set at Mk.¼ – 100°C.

Serves 4
Preparation : 25 minutes
    Cooking : 60 minutes

- 4 large scallops with coral (or 8 small ones)
- 80cl (1½ pints) Bisque d' Homard
- 3 egg yolks + 2 whole eggs
- 20cl (7fl oz) double cream
- salt, freshly ground pepper

Separate the scallops from their corals.

Blend the coral with the double cream.

Heat the Bisque d'Homard without causing it to boil.

Add the coral cream and continue cooking for 2 minutes. Remove from heat and allow to stand for 10 minutes. Reserve a third of the mixture, which will be used later for the sauce.

In a big bowl, beat 2 whole eggs together with 2 yolks. Add the two-thirds of the prepared mixture to the beaten eggs, whipping continuously.

Return to a low heat (or better still to a bain-marie) to thicken the mixture slightly, though it should still remain creamy. Continue stirring all the time with the whisk.

Adjust the seasoning.

Put the scallops into the bottom of 4 small buttered moulds and then fill with the mixture.

Place in an oven (Mk. ½ – 130°C) and cook in a bain-marie for 30 minutes.

Before serving, put the reserved third of the original mixture in a bain-marie. Add the last egg yolk and gently thicken the sauce over a very low heat, stirring constantly with the whisk. Adjust seasoning to taste.

Turn out the ramekins onto warm plates and coat with the sauce.

Gratinées de Saint-Jacques dans leur Coquille

Scallops with Grated Cheese

Serves 4
Preparation : 20 minutes
    Cooking : 20 minutes

- 8 large scallops (12 if medium-sized)
- 4 shells
- 3 chopped shallots
- 1 glass dry white wine
- 4 tablespoons crème fraîche
- 200g (7oz) grated Gruyère cheese
- salt, freshly ground pepper, olive oil, nutmeg

Put a spoonful of olive oil in a casserole. Heat on a low flame. Add chopped shallots and cook until translucent. Do not brown.

Add the white wine. Salt and pepper to taste.

Separate the white of the scallops from their coral. Poach the whites for 1 minute and reserve.

Reduce the wine to a quarter of its original volume. Add the coral, crème fraîche and grated Gruyère and then liquidize.

Arrange the scallops on the shells and cover with the creamy sauce. Add a pinch of nutmeg.

Place under the grill and cook for no more than 4 to 5 minutes, to avoid overcooking the scallops.

Farandole de Poivrons au Bacon
Sweet Pepper Polka with Bacon

Serves 4
Preparation : 20 minutes
    Cooking : 20 minutes

- 2 red peppers
- 2 green peppers
- 2 yellow peppers
- about 20 stoned black olives
- juice of 1 lemon
- 4 cloves garlic – crushed
- 3 tablespoons chopped fresh parsley
- 9 slices bacon (preferably Pancetta)
- 4 tablespoons olive oil
- salt, freshly ground pepper

Cut the sweet peppers into halves. Remove the pith and the seeds.

Place the halved peppers skin side up under the oven grill and cook until the skin starts to char and bubble. Allow to cool and then peel.

Cut the sweet peppers into strips and place in a salad bowl.

Take half the olives and finely chop. Cut the remainder into halves.

With a fork, lightly beat the crushed garlic, lemon juice, olive oil and parsley, salt and freshly ground pepper together. Pour the mixture over the sweet peppers.

Cook the bacon over a low heat until it is completely crunchy. Reserve and allow to cool on absorbent kitchen paper.

Put the dry, crunchy bacon in a mixer and grind to a coarse powder.

Sprinkle the powder over the sweet peppers and serve.

Tomates Farcies à la Semoule Intégrale
Tomatoes Stuffed with Cracked Wheat

Ras-el-hanout is a North African mixture of spices containing cinnamon, nutmeg, dried ginger, cloves and various peppers pounded together.

Serves 4
Preparation : 15 minutes
   Cooking : 60 minutes

- 8 large tomatoes
- 120g (4oz) cracked wheat (Bulghur)
- 10 cloves garlic
- 16 stoned black olives
- 3 tablespoons chopped parsley
- olive oil, salt, freshly ground pepper, cayenne
- pepper, ras-el-hanout

Halve the tomatoes across their segments and hollow out with a spoon. Reserve the pulp in a salad bowl. Arrange the tomatoes on an oven tray and place in a warm oven (Mk.3 – 160°C) for 30 minutes. Reserve.

In a bowl, crush the tomato pulp. Add the crushed cloves of garlic, the puréed stoned black olives, the chopped parsley, 3 tablespoons of olive oil and the unrefined semolina. Add salt, freshly ground pepper, cayenne pepper and a few pinches of the ras-el-hanout. Mix-in well with a spoon and allow to stand for at least an hour.

Fill the tomato halves with the mixture and put back in a warm oven (Mk.3 – 160°C).

Serve hot.

SOUPS

Gaspacho Andalou
Andalousian Gaspacho

Gaspacho is always served very cold with the addition of ice cubes.

Serves 5
Preparation : 15 minutes
    Cooking : 40 minutes

- 1 large cucumber
- 1 courgette
- 2kg (2½lb) tomatoes
- 2 red peppers
- 2 chopped onions
- 5 cloves garlic – crushed
- juice of 3 lemons
- 12 leaves fresh basil
- 5 tablespoons olive oil
- salt, freshly ground pepper, cayenne

Top and tail the courgette and halve lengthways. Cook in a steamer for 30 minutes. Allow to cool.

Top and tail the cucumber and halve lengthways. Remove seeds.

Cover the tomatoes in boiling water for 30 seconds. Pour off water and peel away the split skins. Cut open and remove seeds.

Cut the peppers in half lengthways, remove pith and seeds, place on a tray and put under the grill skin side up until the skin bubbles and chars slightly. Peel.

Liquidize half the cucumber, the courgette, half the peppers, three-quarters of the tomatoes, the onions, garlic, olive oil and the lemon juice. Add salt, freshly ground pepper and cayenne. Liquidize. If the mixture is too thick, thin with tomato juice. Place in the fridge for at least 4 hours.

Before serving, cut rest of the cucumber, tomatoes and peppers into cubes and serve separately as an accompaniment to the gaspacho.

Soupe au Chou
Cabbage Soup

Serves 6
Preparation : 5 minutes
   Cooking : 2 hrs 15 minutes

- 1 large savoy cabbage
- 200g (7oz) smoked bacon
- 300g (10oz) cured ham – thickly sliced
- 200g (7oz) streaky bacon
- 4 small celeriac – diced
- 2 onions
- freshly ground pepper

Fill a large heavy saucepan with 3 litres (6½ pints) of water. Put into it the ham, smoked bacon and streaky bacon.

Bring to the boil. Skim.

Remove any tired leaves from the cabbage. Remove the stem and cut the cabbage into four. Add to the stockpot, together with the diced celeriac and the peeled onions. Season with pepper. Reduce the heat, cover and allow to cook for a good 2 hours.

Take out the meat and half the vegetables, which will make up the main dish later.

Put the remainder (liquid and vegetables) into the blender to make the soup.

Serve very hot.

Velouté Glacé au Concombre
Chilled Cream of Cucumber Soup

Serves 4
Preparation : 10 minutes
No cooking

- 1 good sized cucumber
- 500g (16fl oz) greek yoghurt
- 100g (3oz) finely ground almonds
- 2 cloves garlic – crushed
- 3 tablespoons olive oil
- 20cl (7fl oz) whipping cream
- salt, white pepper
- parsley

Peel the cucumber. Cut along its length. Remove seeds and dice. Sprinkle with salt and drain for 10 minutes. Liquidize.

In a large bowl, mix the cucumber purée, yoghurt, ground almonds, crushed garlic, olive oil and whipping cream. Season with salt and pepper.

Place in a fridge for at least 6 hours.

Serve in chilled plates and sprinkle with freshly chopped parsley.

Velouté d'Ail
Cream of Garlic Soup

Serves 4
Preparation : 20 minutes
     Cooking : 30 minutes

- 4 handsome garlic heads (of approximately 20 cloves)
- 2 courgettes
- 40cl (14fl oz) double cream with 15% fat
- salt, freshly ground pepper, cayenne
- 2 tablespoons olive oil
- 2 tablespoons freshly chopped parsley

Peel the garlic cloves and place on one level of the steamer.

Halve the courgettes, remove the seeds and cut into 3 to 4cm (1½in) cubes. Place on the other level of the steamer.

Cook for 20 minutes.

Put the garlic, courgettes, olive oil and double cream in the mixer, adding salt, freshly ground pepper and cayenne to taste. Liquidize.

Transfer to a pan and reheat gently, adding some milk if necessary, to thin the mixture.

Serve and sprinkle a little chopped parsley on each plate.

Velouté de Poireaux
Cream of Leek Soup

Serves 4
Preparation : 15 minutes
    Cooking : 35 minutes

- 5 or 6 good sized leeks
- 20cl (7fl oz) soya cream
- 1½ chicken stock cubes
- 1 bunch of parsley
- salt and white pepper

Clean the leeks thoroughly and remove most of the green of the leaves.

Cut into pieces 3 to 4cm (1½in) long.

Cook in a steamer for 30 minutes.

In the meantime, prepare 75cl (1½ pints) of chicken stock.

Liquidize the leeks with some of the stock.

Pour the leek purée into the pan containing the stock and add the soya cream. Salt and pepper to taste.

Serve hot and decorate with chopped parsley.

Soupe de Moules à la Crème
Cream of Mussel Soup

Serves 4
Preparation : 15 minutes
    Cooking : 20 minutes

- 1kg (2¼lb) mussels in their shells
- 4 large shallots
- 20cl (7fl oz) dry white wine
- juice of 1 lemon
- 150g (6oz) crème fraîche
- olive oil
- 3 tablespoons chopped fresh parsley
- salt, freshly ground pepper

Clean the mussels in several changes of water and remove the beard.

Discard mussels with broken shells.

Chop the shallots very finely. Brown gently in some olive oil in a large saucepan.

Moisten with the white wine. Season with salt and pepper. Leave to cook for 1 to 2 minutes.

Add the mussels. Cover and cook over a high heat for 5 minutes until the shells have opened.

Take the mussels out of the pot with a slotted spoon and remove from their shells. Reserve and keep warm.

Add lemon juice and parsley to the cooking juices. Add ground pepper and then the cream. Simmer for 3 minutes.

Return the mussels to the liquid, simmer for a further 2 minutes and serve.

Velouté de Crevettes
Cream of Shrimp Soup

Serves 4/5
Preparation : 25 minutes
   Cooking : 30 minutes

- 800g (2 pints) prawns
- 2 onions – finely sliced
- 2 sticks of celery
- 25cl (9fl oz) white wine
- 1 sprig of thyme
- 1 bay leaf
- 150g (5oz) crème fraîche
- 2 egg yolks
- olive oil

Chop the celery sticks into small pieces.

Shell the prawns.

In a covered pan, heat 3 tablespoons of olive oil over a medium heat. Add the onions, celery, thyme and bay leaf. Brown lightly, stirring constantly for 3 to 4 minutes.

Then add the prawns. Continue cooking for 3 minutes.

Pour in the white wine, cover and cook for a further 10 minutes, over a low heat.

Remove the thyme and bay leaf. Put the rest in a mixer and blend. Return to the pan adding 75cl (1¼ pints) of water. Add freshly ground pepper and salt to taste.

Cook over a low heat for about 5 minutes.

Beat the egg yolks and the crème fraîche together in a bowl. Pour the soup gradually into the egg-cream mixture, beating continuously.

Serve in warm bowls.

Crème de Soja aux Echalotes
Cream of Soya with Shallots

Serves 4
Preparation : 15 minutes
   Cooking : 20 minutes

- 10 shallots
- 30cl (10fl oz) dry white wine
- 40cl (14fl oz) soya cream
- olive oil
- fine sea salt
- freshly ground pepper, cayenne
- Herbes de Provence

Cut the shallots into small pieces and put into the blender with 3 tablespoons of olive oil to make a purée.

In a saucepan, heat the purée over a very low flame for 5 or 6 minutes, making sure it does not catch or caramel.

Add the white wine and bring to the boil. Add 1 teaspoon of Herbes de Provence and allow to simmer gently for 5 minutes. Reserve over a low heat.

Add the soya cream, 1 teaspoon of sea salt and 2 pinches of cayenne pepper. Heat for 4 to 5 minutes over a low flame (soya cream can coagulate over a heat that is too high).

Serve hot in soup plates.

Soupe aux Pissenlits
Dandelion Soup

Serves 4
Preparation : 15 minutes
   Cooking : 30 minutes

- 300g (13oz) young dandelion leaves
- 3 small celeriac – diced
- 2 onions
- 6 cloves garlic
- 1 tablespoon goose fat
- 2 tablespoons olive oil
- salt, freshly ground pepper

Wash the dandelion leaves.

Chop the garlic and onion. In a covered saucepan, brown in the olive oil.

Add 75cl (1½ pints) of water and throw in the dandelion leaves and coarsely diced celeriac. Season with salt, pepper and cook on a low heat for 20 minutes.

Pour into a mixer. Add goose fat and liquidize.

Put back into the saucepan. Adjust the seasoning and cook for a further 5 minutes before serving.

Soupe au Pistou
Pistou Soup

Serves 5/6
Preparation : 30 minutes
    Cooking : 1 hr 10 minutes

- 1kg (2¼lb) fresh broad beans (or dried beans that have been soaked overnight)
- 150g (5oz) mangetout
- 300g (10oz) courgettes
- 4 very ripe tomatoes
- 2 large onions
- 4 cloves garlic
- 1 tablespoon chopped fresh basil
- salt, freshly ground pepper
- 150g (5oz) grated Parmesan or Emmental cheese

FOR THE PISTOU:
- 4 very ripe tomatoes
- 4 tablespoons chopped fresh basil
- 5 cloves garlic
- 10cl (3fl oz) olive oil

String and wash the mangetout.

Cut the courgettes in half and into slices of 2 or 3cm (about 1in).

Cut the onions into thin slices and crush the cloves of garlic.

Cover the tomatoes with boiling water for 30 seconds. Take them out, peel, halve and remove the seeds. Chop the flesh coarsely.

Put the beans, courgettes, onions, garlic, tomatoes, mangetout and basil into a large pan. Cover with water. Sprinkle with salt.

Bring to the boil and leave to cook over a low heat for a good hour.

In the meantime, prepare the pistou:

Cover the tomatoes with boiling water, peel, halve, remove the seeds, chop and allow to drain.

Quarter the cloves of garlic.

Liquidize the tomatoes, garlic, basil and olive oil. Season with salt and pepper.

When the soup is ready, add the pistou. Stir, sprinkle the grated cheese on top and serve.

Soupe de Choucroute
Sauerkraut Soup

Serves 4
Preparation : 15 minutes
    Cooking : 60 minutes

- 300g (10oz) sauerkraut
- 75cl (1½ pint) meat stock
- 2 chopped onions
- 1 bay leaf
- 20cl (7fl oz) double cream
- olive oil
- salt, freshly ground pepper

Drain the sauerkraut and then blanch for 10 minutes in boiling water.

In a heavy saucepan, brown the chopped onions in the olive oil over a gentle heat.

Add the sauerkraut and cook until it has coloured slightly. Add a little stock to moisten and then liquidize.

Return the purée to the stockpot and add the rest of the stock and the bay leaf. Allow to cook for a further 40 minutes.

Add the double cream during the last 5 minutes of the cooking. Adjust the seasoning and serve.

Velouté de Concombre au Yaourt Grec Ⓥ
Smooth Cucumber Soup with Greek Yoghurt

Serves 4
Preparation : 20 minutes
No cooking

- 2 cucumbers
- 2 tomatoes
- 500g (16fl oz) Greek Yoghurt
- juice of 2 lemons
- 1 tablespoon olive oil
- 5 leaves fresh mint
- 1 bunch parsley
- salt, freshly ground pepper

Put tomatoes into boiling water and leave for 30 seconds. Quarter, then peel and remove the seeds. Dice finely and reserve.

Peel the cucumber, remove the seeds. Put in a mixer together with the yoghurt, lemon juice, mint, olive oil, salt and pepper. Liquidize.

Transfer the liquid to the fridge and leave for at least 5 hours.

Serve very cold and decorate with the diced tomatoes and freshly chopped parsley.

Velouté de Champignons à la Crème de Soja
Smooth Mushroom Soup with Soya Cream

Serves 4
Preparation : 30 minutes
   Cooking : 1 hr 5 minutes

- 500g (1lb) button mushrooms
- 2 shallots – thinly sliced
- 1 onion – thinly sliced
- 20cl (7fl oz) soya cream
- 1 chicken stock cube
- olive oil
- salt, freshly ground pepper, curry
- a large bunch of parsley

Clean the mushrooms. Cut in half and cook in 1 litre (2 pints) of salted water for 35 minutes.

Reserve the mushrooms and reduce the liquid for 10 minutes after having added the stock cube.

Heat the oil in a saucepan and cook the onion and shallots gently until translucent.

Moisten with the 25cl (9fl oz) of chicken stock. Reduce by simmering for 5 to 10 minutes.

Put the mushrooms in a mixer together with the soya cream and liquidize. Transfer to the saucepan. Warm through over a low heat for 4 to 5 minutes.

Thin if necessary, with the rest of the chicken stock. Season with salt and pepper. Add a pinch of curry.

Serve hot into plates and sprinkle with chopped parsley.

Soupe à l'Oseille
Sorrel Soup

Serves 4
Preparation : 15 minutes
   Cooking : 20 minutes

- 300g (10oz) sorrel
- 15cl (5fl oz) dry white wine
- 2 shallots – finely chopped
- 25cl (9fl oz) chicken stock
- 100g (4oz) crème fraîche
- 2 egg yolks
- salt, freshly ground pepper
- olive oil

Pour 1 tablespoon of olive oil into a heavy saucepan. Lightly brown the shallots over a low heat. Add the wine. Salt and pepper. Simmer and reduce by a third.

Wash the sorrel. Cut the leaves in half and add to the reduced wine. Cover and keep warm.

In another pan, bring the chicken stock to the boil.

In a metal bowl, mix the crème fraîche and the egg yolks together. Add the stock slowly and continue to stir the mixture with a whisk.

Pour the reduced wine and sorrel into the stock. Stir together and check the seasoning.

Keep the soup warm in a bain-marie until ready to serve.

Consommé de Tomates
Tomato Consommé

Serves 4
Preparation : 15 minutes
   Cooking : 25 minutes

- 1kg (2¼lb) tomatoes
- 3 cloves of garlic – crushed
- 3 shallots – chopped
- 2 sprigs of basil
- 2 oregano tips
- salt, freshly ground pepper

Heat a tablespoon of olive oil in a casserole and brown the garlic and shallots over a low heat.

Cover the tomatoes with boiling water and allow to stand for 30 seconds. Then peel and remove the seeds. Cut the flesh into pieces and place in the casserole. Season with salt.

Remove the leaves from the stems of basil and reserve. Chop the basil stems and add to the casserole with the oregano. Raise the temperature and allow to simmer for 10 minutes, partially covering with a lid to reduce spattering.

Liquidize. Adjust salt to taste and add ground pepper and finely chopped basil leaves.

Reheat and serve.

EGGS

Œufs Farcis à la Tapenade
Eggs with Tapenade Stuffing

Serves 4   Phase 2
Preparation : 15 minutes
    Cooking : 10 minutes

- 6 eggs
- 1 small jar (40g or 1½oz) Tapenade, or home made Tapenade –
  see p.246
- 1 tablespoon olive oil
- lettuce leaves
- bunch of parsley

Boil the eggs for 10 minutes until hard. Cool in cold water.

Remove the shell and cut lengthways into two. Scoop out the yolk with a small spoon and place the whites on a serving dish covered with lettuce leaves.

Crush the yolks with a fork and mix with the tapenade and olive oil, to make a smooth paste.

Using the small spoon, fill the whites with the mixture.

Sprinkle freshly chopped parsley over the eggs and serve.

Œufs au Plat et Jambon de Pays
Lightly Fried Eggs and Cured Ham

Serves 4
Preparation : 2 minutes
    Cooking : 10 minutes

- 8 large fresh farm eggs
- 8 slices cured ham cut finely
- goose fat
- salt, freshly ground pepper

In individual pans, cook the eggs in pairs in the goose fat. Do this over a low heat, to ensure the eggs do not crisp and brown at the edges.

Season with sea salt and freshly ground pepper.

Arrange the ham slices on individual plates and serve the eggs on top.

Œufs Mimosa au Thon
Mimosa Eggs with Tuna

Serves 4
Preparation : 15 minutes
    Cooking : 10 minutes

- 6 eggs
- 100g (3½oz) classic mayonnaise
  – preferably home made
- 100g (3½oz) Italian tuna in brine
- 1 tablespoon chopped parsley
- 8 anchovy fillets
- 12 olives

Boil the eggs for 10 minutes until hard. Cool in cold water.

Remove the shell and cut lengthways into two. Scoop out the yolk with a small spoon.

Crush the yolks with a fork to make the mimosa. Reserve.

Drain the tuna and break up with a fork. Mix with the mayonnaise, a quarter of the mimosa and the chopped parsley.

With the small spoon fill the egg whites.

Put 3 filled egg halves on each plate. Sprinkle with the rest of the mimosa. Decorate with the anchovies and olives.

Œufs Pochés à la Provençale
Poached Eggs Provençale

The eggs must be very fresh. Otherwise, when put in the water they will not remain compact.

Serves 4
Preparation : 10 minutes
   Cooking : 15 minutes

- 8 very fresh eggs
- 500g (1lb) puréed tomatoes
- 4 cloves garlic
- 4 tablespoons olive oil
- 1 tablespoon Herbes de Provence
- 1 tablespoon chopped fresh basil
- salt, freshly ground pepper, wine vinegar

In a non-stick pan, cook the puréed tomatoes, crushed cloves of garlic, Herbes de Provence and basil over a low heat.

Season with salt and pepper.

Stir constantly with a wooden spoon to prevent splashing. When the coulis is hot, cover and allow to simmer on a gentle heat.

Boil 2 litres (4 pints) of water together with 2 tablespoons of wine vinegar and ¼ teaspoon of salt.

Break the eggs into a ladle and one by one lower carefully into the boiling water. Immediately reduce the heat and simmer for three and a half minutes. Remove the poached eggs with a slotted spoon and drain on a tea towel. Trim if desired, to improve their appearance.

Add olive oil to the tomato coulis and stir vigorously.

Serve the eggs on hot plates and coat with the tomato coulis.

Œufs Cocotte à l'Estragon
Ramekin Eggs with Tarragon

Serves 4
Preparation : 15 minutes
    Cooking : 18 minutes

- 8 large eggs (very fresh)
- 3 very thin slices cured ham
- 8 tablespoons crème fraîche
- 1 bunch of fresh tarragon

Strip the tarragon and chop finely.

Chop the ham finely.

Butter the ramekins, which should be big enough to accommodate 2 eggs each.

Put half the tarragon in the ramekins. Break the eggs over the top.

In a bowl, mix the crème fraîche, the ham and the rest of the tarragon. Season with salt and pepper.

Pour over the eggs in each ramekin.

Cook au bain-marie for 8 to 10 minutes in a very cool pre-heated oven (Mk. ½ – 130°C).

Œufs Brouillés aux Crevettes
Scrambled Eggs with Prawns

Serves 4
Preparation : 20 minutes
    Cooking : 20 minutes

- 350g (10oz) uncooked prawns
- 6 eggs
- 1 shallot – chopped
- 25cl (9fl oz) dry white wine
- 2 tablespoons chopped dill
- salt, freshly ground pepper
- 1 tablespoon olive oil

Cook the prawns for about 2 minutes in court-bouillon and then shell.

In a frying pan, lightly brown the chopped shallot in the olive oil for about 3 minutes.

Add the white wine. Season with salt and pepper. Reduce by a third. Add the prawns, mix, reserve and keep warm.

Whisk the eggs in a metal bowl. Season with salt and pepper. Cook in a bain-marie, whisking constantly.

Turn out the scrambled eggs on a warm serving dish and decorate with the prawn sauce.

Sprinkle with the dill and serve.

Œufs Brouillés aux Poivrons
Scrambled Eggs with Red Peppers

Serves 4
Preparation : 15 minutes
    Cooking : 25 minutes

- 10 eggs
- 2 red peppers
- Herbes de Provence
- olive oil
- salt, freshly ground pepper, mild paprika

Slice the red peppers lengthways in two. Remove the pith and seeds.

Place the pepper halves under the grill skin side up until slightly charred and bubbled.

Allow to cool and then peel.

Purée the flesh in a mixer.

In a bowl, beat the eggs with the salt, pepper and paprika. Add the pepper purée and mix well.

Cook over a low heat in a pan containing olive oil – or better still, in a bain-marie – continuing to stir all the time.

Dust lightly with the Herbes de Provence and decorate with a trickle of olive oil.

Serve.

Brouillade d'Oseille
Scrambled Eggs with Sorrel

If sorrel is difficult to obtain, substitute with spinach.

Serves 4
Preparation : 15 minutes
    Cooking : 15 minutes

- 300g (12oz) sorrel
- 20cl (7fl oz) double cream
- 4 eggs
- 2 tablespoons crème fraîche
- salt, freshly ground pepper
- olive oil

Wash the sorrel and dry well.

Put olive oil in a deep frying pan or wok. Add the leaves and soften over a very low heat. Add the crème fraîche. Season with salt and pepper.

Reserve and keep warm.

Beat the cream until stiff.

Break the eggs in a large metal bowl. Season with salt and pepper. Beat until frothy.

Put the bowl in a bain-marie and cook, beating constantly.

When the mixture is on the point of setting, incorporate the double cream progressively. Continue cooking.

Lay the sorrel leaves on the plates and pour the eggs over the top.

Brouillade de Truffes
Scrambled Eggs with Truffle Crumbs

Serves 4
Preparation : 15 minutes
    Cooking : 15 minutes

- 10 eggs
- 20g (¾oz) tinned truffle crumbs
- 70g (2½oz) goose fat
- salt, freshly ground pepper

Separate yolks from whites. Put the whites into a large metal bowl and whisk into stiff peaks. Lightly beat the yolks and blend with the whites. Season with salt and pepper. Add the truffle crumbs with their juice.

Put the bowl in a bain-marie and start cooking, stirring constantly with the whisk and progressively adding the goose fat.

When the mixture has set but is still slightly creamy, pour onto a serving dish and serve immediately.

Œufs en Gelée à l'Estragon
Tarragon Eggs in Aspic

The eggs must be very fresh. Otherwise, when put in the water they will not remain compact.

Serves 4
Preparation : 15 minutes
   Cooking : 20 minutes

- 8 very fresh eggs
- 2 slices cooked ham
- 1 packet aspic powder
- 16 leaves of Tarragon
- 10cl (3fl oz) white wine vinegar
- salt, freshly ground pepper

In a large casserole, bring ½ litre (1 pint) of water to the boil.

Add the white wine vinegar, salt and pepper.

Break each egg into a ladle and lower gently into the boiling water to release the egg. Immediately reduce the heat and simmer. Poach the eggs for 3 minutes. Remove with a slotted spoon and drain on a tea towel. Allow to cool.

Prepare the instant aspic as instructed on the packet. Allow to cool slightly and pour ½cm (¼in) of the liquid into the bottom of 8 small moulds (or ramekins).

Place in the freezer for a few minutes so that the aspic can set more quickly.

Place a poached egg in each mould. Then add two leaves of tarragon and a piece of ham the diameter of the mould. Cover with the remainder of the aspic.

Allow to stand in the fridge for 3 hours and then turn out by first dipping the bottom of the moulds into hot water for a few seconds.

Put back in the fridge until required. Serve on a bed of lettuce.

Tortilla à la Montignac
Tortilla Montignac

Serves 4
Preparation : 20 minutes
   Cooking : 15 minutes

- 8 eggs
- 2 onions – finely chopped
- 4 cloves garlic – finely chopped
- 3 courgettes finely sliced
- 3 tablespoons freshly chopped parsley
- 250g (9oz) tomatoes – diced and well drained
- 200g (7oz) Mozzarella
- Herbes de Provence
- olive oil
- salt, freshly ground pepper, cayenne

In a very large frying pan, lightly brown the onion and garlic in the olive oil over a low heat. Add the courgettes and possibly some more olive oil to the pan. Sauté, taking care that the onion and the garlic do not catch.

Beat the eggs and season with salt, pepper and cayenne, adding the chopped parsley.

Pour the eggs into the pan and return to a gentle heat, without stirring.

While the eggs are cooking, sprinkle the tomato cubes evenly over the mixture in the pan.

Preheat the oven grill to Mk.10 – 250°C.

When the tortilla is nearly cooked, sprinkle with Herbes de Provence and spread the finely sliced mozzarella evenly over the top.

Complete the cooking by placing the pan with the tortilla about 10cm (6in) under the grill.

Trickle chilli flavoured olive oil over the top and serve.

Omelette au Thon
Tuna Omelette

Serves 4
Preparation : 15 minutes
　　Cooking : 10 minutes

- 8 eggs
- 200g (7oz) tuna in brine
- 20cl (7fl oz) double cream
- 2 tablespoons freshly chopped parsley
- olive oil

Drain the tuna and mash finely with a fork.

Separate the egg whites and the yolks into different bowls

Whisk the whites into stiff peaks.

Whisk the yolks together with the double cream. Add the tuna and the parsley.

Fold the mixture delicately into the egg whites.

Heat a tablespoon of olive oil in a large pan. Pour in the mixture and cook at normal temperature.

Serve while still slightly moist.

MEAT

Bourguignon
Beef Casserole

Recommended side dishes : Celeriac purée
                          Onion purée

Serves 5
Preparation : 15 minutes
   Cooking : 2 hrs 50 minutes

- 3¼lb chuck steak cut into 4cm (2in) cubes
- 200g (7oz) bacon cubes
- 350g (12oz) mushrooms – sliced
- 25cl (9fl oz) dry red wine (Corbières, Côtes du Rhône, etc)
- 10 pickling onions or shallots
- 25cl (9fl oz) beef stock
- 1 bouquet garni
- 1 sprig parsley
- goose fat

Fry the bacon cubes on a low heat. Add the whole onions until they are lightly browned. Remove and reserve.

In a large casserole heat 3 tablespoons of goose fat. Add the cubes of meat and when they are lightly browned, add the stock.

Then add the bacon cubes and onions to the contents of the casserole. Pour in the red wine. Season with salt, pepper and add the bouquet garni. Cover and leave to cook on a low heat for at least 2 hours.

In a separate pan, cover the sliced mushrooms with a ladleful of stock and cook for 15 minutes. Liquidize half the mushrooms together with some of the cooking fluid. Add to the large casserole, with the rest of the mushrooms.

Allow to cook for 30 minutes with no lid. Remove the bouquet garni, adjust the seasoning, serve in a deep plate and sprinkle with parsley.

Daube Provençale
Beef Casserole Provençale

Recommended side dishes : Celeriac purée
Sweet pepper purée

Serves 5
Preparation : 15 minutes
Cooking : 1 hr 30 minutes

- 1kg (2¼lb) braising steak or chuck steak cut into cubes
- 150g (5oz) streaky bacon – diced
- 4 finely sliced onions
- 30cl (10fl oz) red wine
- 1 bouquet garni
- 20 green olives – stoned
- 20 black olives – stoned
- 75g (3oz) tinned mushrooms
- olive oil, salt, freshly ground pepper

In a casserole, heat 2 tablespoons of olive oil. On a low heat fry the diced bacon and then the sliced onions.

Add the pieces of meat and brown all over. Season with salt and pepper.

Add the bouquet garni and the wine. Cover and allow to simmer for 45 minutes.

Strain the mushrooms and transfer to a liquidizer. Add a tablespoon of the cooking fluid and purée.

Add the mushroom purée and olives to casserole. Cover and continue cooking over a low heat for 30 minutes. Remove the cover and cook for a further 30 minutes.

Serve hot after removing the bouquet garni.

Blanquette de Veau à la Montignac
Blanquette of Veal Montignac

As this dish contains a lot of vegetables, it should be served as a dish on its own.

Serves 5
Preparation : 30 minutes
    Cooking : 1 hr 15 minutes

- 1.5kg (3¼lb) shoulder of veal, with no fat or bone, cut into 2cm (1in) cubes
- 1kg (2¼lb) button mushrooms
- 8 leeks
- 3 onions
- 4 cloves garlic
- 1 bouquet garni
- 1.5 litres (3 pints) veal stock
- 40cl (14fl oz) double cream
- 2 egg yolks
- juice of 2 lemons
- 3 tablespoons chopped fresh parsley
- goose fat

Prepare the vegetables: wash and cut the leeks into rings, clean the mushrooms and slice. Slice the onions and garlic thinly.

Put goose fat into a pan with a lid and brown the pieces of meat over a gentle heat. Season with salt and pepper.

Put all the vegetables on top of the meat as well as the bouquet garni.

Pour the stock over the top and bring to the boil. Then turn down the heat, cover and allow to cook gently for an hour and a quarter.

Using a slotted spoon, remove half of the mushrooms, leeks and onions. Drain them well and put them into a blender to make a purée.

Transfer the purée into a casserole together with the double cream. Add 2 egg yolks and stir continuously with the whisk for several minutes. When the cream begins to thicken, remove from the heat and continue to stir for 1 or 2 minutes.

Take the pan with the meat and pour off three quarters of the stock, to leave the meat, vegetables and a small amount of cooking liquid. Remove the bouquet garni.

Pour the sauce over the top and mix well, leaving the blanquette to stand in a warm place to ensure it maintains its temperature without cooking further.

Serve on warm plates.

Foie de Veau au Basilic
Calf's Liver with Basil

Recommended side dishes according to season : Ratatouille
Braised chicory
Provençale tomatoes

Serves 4
Preparation : 5 minutes
Cooking : 10 minutes

- 4 slices calf's liver
  each slice about 170g (6oz)
- 20 leaves basil – chopped
- 4 cloves garlic – crushed
- olive oil
- salt, freshly ground pepper

Mix the crushed garlic, the chopped basil and 3 dessert spoons of olive oil.

Put this mixture in a big frying pan and cook for 3 minutes on a very gentle heat.

Add the slices of veal and cook on each side over a medium heat for 3 minutes.

Serve on a warm plate.

Foie de Veau aux Oignons
Calf's Liver with Onions

Serves 4
Preparation : 15 minutes
   Cooking : 15 minutes

- 4 slices calf's liver (170g or 6oz each)
- 10 large onions
- olive oil
- goose fat
- 10cl (4oz) double cream
- 1 tablespoon balsamic vinegar
- salt, freshly ground pepper

Slice the onions.

Heat a small amount of olive oil in a large non-stick fryingpan. Add the onions. Then season with salt and pepper. Do not brown the onions, but cook until almost transparent.

In another frying pan, cook the slices of liver in the goose fat. Season with salt, pepper, reserve and keep warm.

Deglaze the second fryingpan with the balsamic vinegar and the double cream. Add the cooked onions and stir well into the mixture.

Serve on warm plates, coating the liver with the onion sauce.

Gigot à l'Anglaise
English Leg of Lamb – French Style

Recommended side dishes : Broccoli
French beans

Serves 5
Preparation : 15 minutes
Cooking : 60 minutes

- 1½kg (3¼lb) leg of lamb
- 2 bunches mint
- 1 tablespoon fructose
- 1 glass cider vinegar
- goose fat
- salt, freshly ground pepper, cayenne

Grease the roasting tin with goose fat.

Cover the bottom of the tin with mint leaves.

Brush the leg liberally with goose fat. Season with salt, pepper and dust very lightly with cayenne all over.

Cook in the oven (Mk.5 – 190°C) for 1 hour 30 or 40 minutes, depending on how pink you prefer your lamb.

While the meat is cooking, chop finely two dozen leaves of mint.

Boil the cider vinegar in a pan together with the chopped mint for 2 minutes. Turn off the heat and allow to cool for 3 minutes. Add the fructose, stirring well to ensure that it dissolves completely. Liquidize. Then place in the fridge to chill. Remove the leg of lamb from the oven and carve in the tin, to ensure none of the juices are lost. Then arrange the meat on a hot serving dish.

Deglaze the cooking tin with a glass of boiling salted water and pour into a sauce boat.

Serve the meat at the same time as the mint sauce and the deglazed cooking juices.

Entrecôtes à la Bordelaise
Entrecote Steaks Bordeaux Style

Recommended side dishes : Mushrooms with parsley
French beans

Serves 4
Preparation : 15 minutes
Cooking : 30 minutes

- 2 entrecote steaks weighing 500g and 4cm thick (16oz and 2in thick)
- 20cl (7fl oz) red Bordeaux wine
- 10cl (3½fl oz) strong meat stock
- 100g (3½oz) tinned button mushrooms
- 5 shallots – chopped
- 4 tablespoons goose fat
- 1 sprig thyme
- 2 bay leaves
- 1 bunch of chopped parsley
- salt and freshly ground pepper

In a casserole heat 2 tablespoons of goose fat. Fry the shallots lightly for 2 to 3 minutes. Add a little red wine to moisten and then add the thyme, bay leaves and stock. Season with salt and pepper. Over a strong heat with the lid removed, reduce the liquid by half.

Drain the mushrooms, place in a liquidizer with a little olive oil and reduce to a purée. Add this purée to the sauce in the casserole.

In a large frying pan, heat the rest of the goose fat. Add the steaks and sear on both sides. Season with salt and pepper, and cook until the meat is either rare, medium or well done, according to individual taste.

Deglaze the fryingpan with a little red wine. Add the deglazing to the sauce.

Cut the steaks into 4 or 8 slices and arrange on a warm serving dish. Cover with the bordelaise sauce and serve.

Noix de Veau Provençale
Fillet of Veal Provençale

Recommended side dishes : Courgettes gratin
Provençale tomatoes
Ratatouille

Serves 5
Preparation : 25 minutes
   Cooking : 1 hr 15 minutes

- 1.5kg (3¼lb) fillet of veal
- 2 large onions – sliced
- 4 large tomatoes
- 100g (3oz) tomato purée
- 4 cloves garlic
- 100g (3oz) stoned green olives
- 1 glass white wine
- 200g (7oz) pickling onions or shallots
- chopped parsley
- olive oil
- salt, pepper

Cut the meat into cubes of about 4cm (2in).

In a casserole, brown the veal on all sides in 3 tablespoons of olive oil. Season with salt and pepper. Reserve the veal on a separate dish.

In the same casserole, brown the onions over a low heat.

Pour boiling water over the tomatoes and leave for 30 seconds. Remove the skins and the seeds. Then dice the pulp and throw the pieces into the casserole together with the crushed garlic. Cook over a low heat for 5 minutes.

In a bowl, mix the tomato purée with the glass of white wine and 1 tablespoon of olive oil. Then pour into the casserole.

Skin the small onions and cook in a pan of salted water for 30 minutes.

Return the veal to the casserole together with the onions and the olives. Stir well and cover, cooking over a very gentle heat for 30 minutes. Add a little wine if necessary while cooking, to prevent the meat catching on the bottom of the pan.

Correct seasoning.

Arrange on a warm serving dish, sprinkle with parsley and serve.

Emincé de Veau
Goujons of Veal

Recommended side dishes : Braised chicory
Extra thin French beans

Serves 4
Preparation : 20 minutes
Cooking : 25 minutes

- 4 thick veal escalopes cut into ribbons (goujons)
- 200g (7oz) button mushrooms
- 3 onions – finely sliced
- 30cl (10fl oz) double cream
- juice of 1 lemon
- goose fat
- salt, freshly ground pepper, nutmeg
- olive oil

Clean the mushrooms and slice. Brown over a low heat in a frying pan with olive oil. Season with salt and pepper. Throw away the water that has seeped out of the mushrooms and add a little olive oil.

Fry the onions in some olive oil over a low heat.

Melt 1 tablespoon of goose fat in a casserole. Over a low heat, brown the veal goujons, turning constantly. Season with salt, pepper and add the lemon juice.

Add the button mushrooms and onions. Stir. Pour over the double cream and grate the nutmeg on top.

Stir together well and leave to cook on a very gentle heat with the lid off, for 2 or 3 minutes. Taste and adjust the seasoning.

Gigot d'Agneau au Romarin
Leg of Lamb with Rosemary

Recommended side dishes : Flageolet beans
French beans

Serves 4/5
Preparation : 10 minutes
    Cooking : 1 hr 30 minutes

- 2kg (4½lb) leg of lamb
- 6 cloves garlic – crushed
- 1 large sprig rosemary
- 1 tablespoon of sea salt
- freshly ground pepper
- cayenne
- goose fat

In a large bowl, mix garlic purée, crumbled rosemary, salt, 2 tablespoons of softened goose fat and 3 large pinches of cayenne.

Rub the mixture well into the leg of lamb. Put it into a roasting tin with the fatty side uppermost and roast (Mk.5 – 190°C) for 1 hour 50 minutes.

Melt 3 tablespoons of goose fat in 10cl (4fl oz) of boiling water, basting the leg every 15 minutes.

Filet de Mouton à la Provençale
Mutton Fillet Provençale

Recommended side dishes : Ratatouille
                          Haricot beans

Serves 5
Preparation : 15 minutes
   Cooking : 30 minutes

- 1kg (2¼lb) mutton fillet or saddle – boned
  (If mutton is unavailable, substitute with lamb)
- 2 onions – finely sliced
- 2 cloves garlic – crushed
- 20cl (7fl oz) beef stock
- 200g (7oz) tomato purée
- olive oil
- Herbes de Provence
- salt, freshly ground pepper

Cut the meat into 3cm (1in) cubes.

Pour 2 tablespoons of olive oil into a casserole. Add onions and brown over a low heat. Then brown the cubes of mutton on all sides. Add the garlic and a couple of teaspoons of Herbes de Provence. Season with salt and pepper.

In a separate pan, slowly thin the tomato purée with the hot stock. Add salt and pepper to taste.

Pour the tomato sauce into the casserole and mix well. Add 2 tablespoons of olive oil. With the lid on, continue cooking over a very low heat until the meat is just pink. Serve hot.

Côtes de Porc à la Moutarde
Pork Chops with Cream of Mustard Sauce

Recommended side dishes : Celeriac purée
　　　　　　　　　　　　　French beans

Phase 2

Serves 4
Preparation : 10 minutes
　Cooking : 25 minutes

- 4 large pork chops (or 8 small chops)
- 80g (3oz) crème fraîche
- 3 tablespoons strong French mustard
- 1 tablespoon capers (preferably salted)
- 1 tablespoon goose fat

In a bowl, mix the crème fraîche, mustard and rinsed capers.

Over a medium to high heat, melt the goose fat in a large frying pan and brown the chops for about 7 to 8 minutes on each side. Season with salt and pepper.

Pour the sauce over the chops. Cover the pan and allow to simmer for about 10 minutes.

Serve on warm plates.

Grillades de Porc Provençales
Pork Shoulder Chops Provençale

Recommended side dishes : Courgettes gratin
Provençale tomatoes
Ratatouille

Serves 4
Preparation : 15 minutes
  Cooking : 15 minutes

- 4 pork shoulder chops
- 4 shallots – sliced
- 20cl (7fl oz) white wine
- 3 or 4 tablespoons tomato purée
- olive oil, goose fat
- Herbes de Provence
- salt, freshly ground pepper

Heat 2 tablespoons of olive oil in a frying pan. Over a low heat brown the shallots. Moisten with a little white wine and cook for 5 minutes, stirring occasionally.

Thin the tomato purée with the remainder of the wine. Add to the pan with a tablespoon of olive oil. Season with salt and pepper. Put aside and keep warm over a very, very low heat.

Sprinkle Herbes de Provence over the chops.

In a fryingpan, heat a generous tablespoon of goose fat. Add the chops and cook over a low heat, browning first on one side then on the other. Season with salt and pepper.

Arrange the chops on a warm plate and coat with the sauce.

Carré d'Agneau à la Provençale
Rack of Lamb Provençale

Serves 4
Preparation : 25 minutes
   Cooking : 45 minutes

- 1 rack of lamb, weighing about 1kg (2¼lb)
- (8 good-size chops)
- 10cl (4fl oz) dry white wine
- 15cl (5fl oz) crème fraîche
- 1 tablespoon cognac
- 5 cloves garlic – peeled
- olive oil
- Herbes de Provence
- 400g (14oz) button mushrooms
- salt, freshly ground pepper, cayenne
- 1 tablespoon of chopped parsley

Cut 2 cloves of garlic into a total of 8 slices. Make deep gashes in the rack of lamb (between each chop) and insert the slivers of garlic,

Coat the cooking tin with olive oil.

Mix 4 tablespoons of olive oil together with salt, pepper and a pinch of cayenne.

Place the rack of lamb in the tin and brush with the seasoned olive oil. Sprinkle with the Herbes de Provence and place in a very hot oven (Mk.10 – 250°C). Cook for 20 to 25 minutes.

In the meantime, clean the mushrooms and remove the stalks. Cut into slices – the stalks down their length.

Brown the mushrooms over a very gentle heat, in a pan with olive oil. Season with salt and pepper. After a few minutes, remove the cooking juices and water they have produced.

Crush the 3 remaining cloves of garlic and mix them with the parsley. Add them to the mushrooms in the olive oil. Continue cooking over a gentle heat for several minutes, stirring well.

Take the rack of lamb out of the oven and cut it up in the cooking tin. Reserve the chops and keep warm.

Deglaze the tin with the white wine and cognac that have already been heated. Add the crème fraîche and pour into a warm sauceboat.

Serve the rack on a warm plate surrounded with mushrooms.

Rôti de Porc au Curry
Roast Pork with Curry

Recommended side dishes : Brussel sprouts
Broccoli
French beans

Serves 4
Preparation : 15 minutes
Cooking : 1 hr 15 minutes

- 1.8kg (4lb) pork fillet
- 4 cloves garlic – skinned
- 3 tablespoons goose fat
- 20cl (7fl oz) double cream
- curry
- salt, freshly ground pepper

With a sharp pointed knife, make 4 deep cuts in the meat. Push the cloves of garlic deep into the flesh.

In a bowl, prepare a marinade with the melted goose fat. Season with salt, pepper and 1 tablespoon of curry. Mix well.

Rub the mixture well into the meat.

Place the meat in a tin and pour around the meat the rest of the marinade together with ½ glass of water. Roast in the oven (Mk.7 – 220°C) for 1 hour 15 minutes.

Before serving, deglaze the tin with the double cream.

Rôti de Veau aux Olives
Roast Veal with Olives

Serves 4/5
Preparation : 20 minutes
  Cooking : 1 hr 45 minutes

- joint of veal weighing about 1.2kg (2½lb)
- 100g (4oz) streaky bacon – diced
- 200g (7oz) black olives – stone
- 200g (7oz) green olives – stoned
- 15cl (5fl oz) white wine
- salt, freshly ground pepper, thyme

In a casserole fry the diced streaky bacon over a gentle heat. Add the veal and brown lightly all over. Season with salt, pepper and sprinkle with a few pinches of thyme. Cover and cook over a very gentle heat.

Combine 1 tablespoon of olive oil with 75g green olives and 75g black olives in a blender (3oz each) and reduce to a purée. Pour into the casserole and stir in the wine.

Leave to cook over a very gentle heat for 1 hour, turning the meat from time to time.

Add the rest of the olives and allow to cook for a further 20 to 30 minutes, always over a low heat.

Take the roast out of the casserole. Slice and arrange on a warm dish and garnish with the olives.

Pour off the juices and set aside. Deglaze the residue on the bottom of the casserole with a little boiling water. Add the juices and stir.

Pour into a sauceboat and serve.

Roulés d'Escalope au Jambon à la Provençale
Rolled Escalopes with Ham Provence Style

Recommended side dishes : Aubergines with olive oil
Courgette gratin
Mange-tout

Serves 4
Preparation : 20 minutes
    Cooking : 20 minutes

- 8 thin slices pork or veal
- 8 thin slices cured ham
- 3 tablespoons tomato paste
- 100g (4oz) shallots – chopped
- 3 cloves garlic – chopped
- 5cl (2fl oz) brandy
- thyme
- goose fat, olive oil
- salt, freshly ground pepper

Sprinkle the thyme on one side of each escalope. Having first removed the rind and the fat, lay a slice of ham on top of each escalope. Roll and secure with string.

In a casserole heat 1 tablespoon of goose fat, brown the rolls of meat until golden.

At the same time, in a frying pan with a little olive oil, brown the sliced shallots and garlic over a gentle heat.

In a bowl, add 10cl of water (4fl oz) and a tablespoon of olive oil to the tomato purée. Season with salt and pepper.

Put the tomato paste, shallots and garlic in the casserole. Stir and cook over a gentle heat for 2 or 3 minutes.

Note: This dish can be kept hot and allowed to stand for a good quarter of an hour before serving.

Echine de Porc à l'Andalouse
Spare Rib of Pork Andalousia

Serves 4
Preparation : 15 minutes
   Cooking : 1 hr 15 minutes

- 800g (1¾lb) boned spare rib of pork
- 100g (4oz) streaky bacon – diced
- 800g (1¾lb) celeriac – peeled and washed
- 100g (4oz) black olives – stoned
- 100g (4oz) green olives – stoned
- 3 to 4 tablespoons tomato purée
- 1 glass port
- salt, freshly ground pepper, olive oil

In a casserole heat some olive oil and fry the cubes of streaky bacon over a gentle heat.

Cut the celeriac into cubes of 3cm (1in). Blanch for 3 minutes in salted boiling water. Drain well.

Cut the pork into pieces. Lightly brown over a low heat in the casserole for about 10 minutes, in the bacon fat. Season with salt, pepper, then add the celeriac, olives and the tomato paste. Pour over the port and stir.

Cover the casserole and leave to cook on a low heat for 1 hour.

Tournedos à la Provençale
Tournedos Provençale

Serves 4
Preparation : 15 minutes
    Cooking : 40 minutes

- 4 tournedos cut from the fillet, about 200g (8oz) each
- 6 nice tomatoes
- 2 onions – sliced
- 3 red peppers
- 3 cloves garlic – finely sliced
- olive oil, goose fat
- salt, freshly ground pepper
- Herbes de Provence

Cut the red peppers in half down their length. Remove the stalk and the seeds. Place under the grill skin-side up. When the skin has bubbled and is slightly charred, put them on one side to cool.

Remove the skin and cut into strips about 1cm (½in) thick .

Plunge the tomatoes into boiling water for about 30 seconds. Skin, deseed and cut into small cubes.

In a large fryingpan heat 2 or 3 tablespoons of olive oil over a low heat. Brown the onions stirring frequently. Add the garlic, diced tomatoes and strips of red pepper.

Season with salt and pepper, and sprinkle a few Herbes de Provence sparingly over the top. Leave to cook over a gentle heat for 20 minutes.

In another frying pan, melt a nob of goose fat and brown the tournedos 2 or 3 minutes each side. Season with salt and pepper.

Pour the tomato sauce over the meat and continue cooking for 2 minutes.

Serve hot.

Tournedos aux Olives
Tournedos with Olives

Serves 4
Preparation : 15 minutes
    Cooking : 25 minutes

- 4 tournedos – 200g (8oz) each
- 4 large tomatoes
- 20 stoned black olives
- 4 tablespoons anchovy paste
- olive oil
- salt, freshly ground pepper, Herbes de Provence

Cut each of the tomatoes into three. Place in an ovenware dish and brush with oil on both sides. Season with salt, pepper and sprinkle with Herbes de Provence.

Put under the grill until they are slightly browned. Reserve and keep warm.

In a frying pan, fry the black olives in the olive oil. Add the tomatoes.

Brush the tournedos with the anchovy paste. Heat some olive oil in a frying pan and cook the meat for 2 or 3 minutes on each side. Do not salt.

Serve the tournedos very hot with the tomatoes, olives and their cooking juices.

Côtes de Veau Provençales
Veal Chops Provençale

Serves 4
Preparation : 15 minutes
 Cooking : 25 minutes

- 4 veal chops, with fat removed
  approximate weight 200g (8oz) each
- 2 onions – finely sliced
- 3 garlic cloves – crushed
- 2 tablespoons freshly chopped basil
- 1 tablespoon freshly chopped parsley
- 3 tablespoons tomato purée
- white wine
- goose fat, olive oil
- Herbes de Provence
- salt, freshly ground pepper

In a casserole heat 2 tablespoons of olive oil. Brown the onions over a low heat and when cooked, add the crushed garlic.

Add the tomato paste thinned with a little white wine to make it smooth and creamy. Season with salt, pepper and add the fresh basil. Reserve and keep warm.

Season the veal chops and dust them with the Herbes de Provence.

Melt 1 tablespoon of goose fat in a frying pan and fry the veal chops gently over a medium heat – 7 to 8 minutes each side. Remove to a serving dish and keep warm.

Pour away the fat from the cooking juices and deglaze the pan with ½ glass of white wine. Add the tomato paste. Turn off the heat and add a tablespoon of olive oil.

Coat the veal chops with the sauce and sprinkle with parsley.

Côtes de Veau à la Fondue d'Oseille
Veal Chops with Sorrel Fondue

Serves 4
Preparation : 15 minutes
    Cooking : 15 minutes

- 4 veal chops, with fat removed –
  approximate weight 200g (8oz) each
- 150g (5oz) finely chopped sorrel
- juice of 1 lemon
- goose fat, olive oil
- salt, freshly ground pepper

In a large frying pan, melt 1 tablespoon of goose fat over a gentle heat.

Put in the veal chops and brown for 5 to 7 minutes on each side. Season with salt and pepper, then reserve.

While the chops are cooking, remove the stalks from the sorrel and wash well. Dry with a tea towel or kitchen paper.

Pour 2 tablespoons of olive oil into a casserole and add the finely chopped sorrel. Cook gently on a low heat, stirring with a wooden spoon for about 5 minutes. Salt and pepper lightly.

Remove and throw away the excess fat from the cooking juices of the veal. Deglaze the bottom of the frying pan with the lemon juice, add the sorrel fondue and then the chops. Mix well and continue cooking over a low heat for 1 or 2 minutes.

Arrange on a serving dish, dribble olive oil over the top and serve.

Escalope de Veau à la Crème de Parme
Veal Escalope with Parma Cream

Recommended side dishes : Extra thin French beans
                          Mangetout

Serves 4
Preparation : 15 minutes
    Cooking : 35 minutes

- 4 escalopes weighing about 600g (1¼lb)
- 6 slices Parma ham
- 1 onion
- 15cl (5fl oz) crème fraîche
- 1 tablespoon olive oil
- goose fat

In a non-stick frying pan, cook the slices of Parma ham over a low heat (1 to 2 minutes on each side), making sure they are in overall contact with the bottom of the pan.

Dry them in the oven (Mk. ½ – 130°C) until completely stiff and brittle. Cut into pieces and reduce to a powder in the blender. Reserve.

Slice the onion finely and fry in a little olive oil over a low heat. Add the Parma ham powder and the crème fraîche. Season with salt, pepper and a pinch of cayenne.

Salt and pepper the escalopes. Melt the goose fat in a frying pan and gently fry the escalopes.

To serve, arrange on a dish or even better, serve on individual warmed plates and coat with the Parma Cream.

Veau au Paprika
Veal with Paprika

Recommended side dishes : Braised chicory
Cauliflower gratin

Serves 4
Preparation : 15 minutes
Cooking : 1 hr 10 minutes

- 1kg (2¼lb) fillet of veal
- 6 large onions – sliced
- 20cl (7fl oz) crème fraîche
- 20cl (7fl oz) white wine
- goose fat
- olive oil
- 1 bouquet garni
- mild paprika
- hot paprika
- salt, freshly ground pepper

In a frying pan, fry the onions in olive oil over a gentle heat.

Cut the meat into cubes of 3 or 4cm (1½in). Heat the goose fat in a casserole and brown the meat on all sides.

Put the onions in the casserole. Add the white wine, bouquet garni, 3 teaspoons of mild paprika, 1 teaspoon of hot paprika, salt and pepper. Stir well, cover the casserole and cook over a gentle heat for at least an hour.

Remove the pieces of meat, arrange on a serving dish and keep warm. Discard the bouquet garni.

Transfer the rest to a liquidizer and reduce to a creamy sauce.

Add the crème fraîche and mix well.

Pour the sauce over the top of the meat and serve immediately.

POULTRY

Chapon aux Pruneaux, Sauce au Cognac
Capon with Prunes and Cognac Sauce

Serves 6/8   (Phase 2)
Preparation : 30 minutes
    Cooking : 2 hrs 45 minutes

- 1 large capon about 3.5kg (8lb)
- 6 slices bacon
- 250g (9oz) diced streaky bacon
- 2 onions – sliced
- 3 eggs
- 3 slices toasted wholemeal bread, preferably pain intégrale
- 1 tablespoon goose fat
- 40cl (14fl oz) double cream
- 30 stoned prunes
- 10cl (4fl oz) brandy
- 1 sprig tarragon
- ½ teaspoon Herbes de Provence
- salt, freshly ground pepper, cayenne
- olive oil
- 20cl (7fl oz) white wine

Fry the streaky bacon. When there is sufficient melted fat in the pan, add the onions and brown.

In a bowl, mix the diced bacon, onions, 20cl (7fl oz) double cream, eggs and crumbs made from the toasted bread.

Season generously with salt, pepper and cayenne. Add chopped tarragon, Herbes de Provence. Mix well with a fork or in the blender. Fill the capon with stuffing.

Using the point of a knife, raise the skin of the capon and slide in the bacon slices to cover the carcass.

Melt the goose fat over a very, very low heat and then brush liberally over the capon.

Put the capon into a large tin and cook in the oven (Mk.6 – 200°C) for 2 hours and 15 minutes.

Gently simmer the prunes in the white wine for 15 minutes. Drain and arrange in the cooking tin around the capon about 20 minutes before cooking is completed.

Take the capon out of the oven. Pour off about three quarters of the fat in the pan. Add the brandy and flambé.

Carve the capon in the tin to conserve the juices. Then deglaze with the remaining 20cl (7fl oz) of double cream.

Arrange the pieces of capon on a warm plate, surrounded by the prunes. Reheat the sauce and pour into the sauceboat.

Serve immediately.

Blancs de Poulet à la Crème d'Ail
Chicken Breasts in creamy garlic sauce

Recommended side dishes : Ratatouille
Provençale tomatoes

Serves 4
Preparation : 20 minutes
Cooking : 60 minutes

- 4 boneless chicken breasts
- 2 heads garlic
- 30cl (10fl oz) soya cream
- goose fat
- salt, freshly ground pepper, mild paprika
- cayenne
- 1 bunch parsley

Break up the heads of garlic, peel the cloves and cook in a steamer **for 30 minutes.**

Place the chicken breasts in an ovenware dish and brush with goose fat. Season with salt, pepper and sprinkle lightly with cayenne.

Put in the oven (Mk.5 – 190°C) for 20 to 25 minutes.

Liquidize the garlic cloves with the soya cream. Season with salt, pepper and add the equivalent of ½ teaspoon of mild paprika.

Remove the chicken breasts from the oven and cut widthways in 1 to 2cm (½in) slices. Rearrange in the cooking dish.

Coat with the garlic cream and leave in a lukewarm oven (100°C) for 10 to 15 minutes.

Sprinkle with chopped parsley and serve.

Blancs de Poulet en Papillote à l'Estragon
Chicken Breasts and Tarragon in a Bag

Serves 4
Preparation : 20 minutes
Cooking : 15 minutes

- 4 boneless chicken breasts
- 2 tomatoes
- ½ bunch fresh tarragon
- juice of 1 lemon
- 4 tablespoons olive oil
- salt, freshly ground pepper, cayenne
- 1 teaspoon strong mustard

Cut the tomatoes into thick slices. Salt on both sides and leave to degorge on absorbent kitchen paper.

Pre-heat the oven (Mk.10 – 250°C).

Prepare the tarragon, choosing the best leaves.

Cut each chicken breast into 5 or 6 pieces and arrange in a bag made from kitchen foil, together with a couple of slices of tomato and the tarragon leaves.

Sprinkle with 1 tablespoon of olive oil and the juice of a ¼ lemon. Season with salt, pepper, add a pinch of cayenne and close the bag. Put in the oven to cook for 15 minutes.

When ready, open the bags, pour off the liquid. Mix the liquid with the mustard (Phase 2). Serve the chicken in the bag and pour over the sauce.

Emincés de Blanc de Poulet au Curry
Chicken Breasts with Curry Sauce

Serves 5
Preparation : 20 minutes
   Cooking : 35 minutes

- 5 boneless chicken breasts
- 3 large onions – sliced
- 500g (1lb) button mushrooms
- 30cl (10fl oz) fat reduced (15%) double cream or soya cream
- goose fat
- olive oil
- 3 teaspoons curry powder
- salt, pepper, mild paprika, Herbes de Provence

Fry the onions in some olive oil.

Clean the mushrooms, slice and cook in a steamer for 20 minutes.

Cut the chicken breasts into slices 2cm (1in) thick.

Stir fry the chicken over a low heat in a little goose fat. Season with salt, mild paprika, pepper and dust with Herbes de Provence.

Ensure the chicken goujons stay white and evenly cooked.

Add the onions and the mushrooms to the chicken, followed by the cream and the 3 teaspoons of curry powder. Stir well and cover, cooking on a very, very low heat for 5 minutes.

Adjust the seasoning, bearing in mind individual preferences as far as the spicyness of curry is concerned.

Blancs de Poulet au Citron Vert
Chicken Breasts with Lime

Recommended side dishes : Extra fine French beans
Broccoli

Serves 4
Preparation : 15 minutes
  Cooking : 45 minutes

- 4 boneless chicken breasts
- 5 garlic cloves – crushed
- 3 limes
- 4 tablespoons olive oil
- salt, freshly ground pepper, cayenne

In a bowl, make a marinade of lime juice, olive oil, crushed garlic, salt and pepper.
Mix well.

Dust the chicken breasts lightly with cayenne and immerse in the marinade.

Place in the fridge for a few hours, turning from time to time.

Drain the chicken breasts and put them in a roasting tin. Place in a preheated oven
(Mk.5 – 190°C) and cook for 30 minutes.

In the meantime, pour the marinade into a pan, bring to the boil and reduce to obtain
a thick sauce.

Serve the chicken breasts coated with this sauce.

Blancs de Poulet à la Provençale
Chicken Breasts Provençale

Recommended side dish : Green salad

Serves 4
Preparation : 10 minutes
   Cooking : 15 minutes

- 4 boneless chicken breasts
- 500g (18oz) fresh tomato purée
  or 250g (9oz) tomato paste + 25cl (9fl oz) water
- 1 tablespoon Herbes de Provence
- 4 tablespoons olive oil
- 4 cloves garlic crushed
- salt, pepper, cayenne

Cut the chicken breasts into slices 2cm (1in) thick. Salt and sprinkle with cayenne.

Cook in a steamer for 5 minutes

Meanwhile, pour the tomato purée into a casserole. Add the the garlic, the Herbes de Provence and the 4 tablespoons of olive oil. Salt and pepper. Stir and .put back on a very gentle heat.

Turn the chicken breasts (with pink centres) into the casserole. Stir well, cover and cook over an extremely low heat for 5 minutes with the lid on. Correct the seasoning before serving.

Variation: If desired, trickle a little olive oil over the chicken when served.

This dish can be prepared in advance and gently re-heated with the lid on.

Coq au Vin
Chicken Casserole in Wine

Recommended side dishes : Celeriac purée
                         Onion purée

Serves 4
Preparation : 30 minutes
   Cooking : 1 hr 10 minutes

- 1 large freerange chicken
- 2 onions – chopped
- 2 cloves garlic
- 100g (4oz) diced streaky bacon
- 400g (14oz) tinned mushrooms
- 50cl (18fl oz) red wine with a high tannin content,
  like Corbières, Côtes du Rhône . . .
- 2 tablespoons goose fat
- salt, freshly ground pepper, cayenne

Cut the chicken up into several pieces and remove most of the skin.

Melt the goose fat in a casserole. Lightly brown the onions and garlic over a gentle heat.

In the meantime, brown the diced streaky bacon in a non-stick pan until most of the fat has melted.

Fry the chicken pieces in the casserole until golden brown. Add the streaky bacon without the melted fat and add a little red wine.

Season with salt, pepper and cayenne. Raise the temperature and bring to the boil. Reduce the heat and simmer.

Drain the mushrooms. Put half in the liquidizer with a little wine and make a purée. Add to the contents of the casserole, together with the rest of the mushrooms.

Stir and simmer for an hour. Adjust the seasoning. Allow to cool.

Slowly reheat the coq-au-vin and serve.

Poulet en Croûte de Sel
Chicken in a Salt Crust

Recommended side dishes : Braised chicory
Cauliflower gratin
Courgette gratin

Serves 4
Preparation : 10 minutes
Cooking : 1 hr 40 minutes

- 1 free-range chicken weighing about 1.4kg (3lb)
- 2 to 3kg (5-6lb) coarse salt
- 30cl (10fl oz) double cream
- 1 chicken stock cube

In a cast iron stock-pot big enough to take the chicken with ease, lay a bed of salt 2cm (1in) thick .

Lay the chicken on top and cover with salt, to a depth of 1.5cm (½in).

Place in a pre-heated oven (Mk.4 – 180°C) and cook for 1 hour 30 minutes.

Crack the crust and take out the chicken when it will be ready to serve and eat.

As there are no cooking juices, a sauce may be prepared by dissolving 1 cube of chicken stock in 30cl (10fl oz) of whipping cream. To ensure the cube dissolves properly, grate it into a powder with the blade of a serrated knife. Avoid overheating the cream.

Foies de Volaille à la Purée de Céleri
Chicken Livers with Celeriac Purée

Serves 4
Preparation : 15 minutes
    Cooking : 1 hr 15 minutes

- 600g (1¼lb) chicken livers
- 1 celeriac
- 1 lemon, cut into quarters
- 30cl (10fl oz) double cream
- 2 tablespoons balsamic vinegar
- goose fat
- salt, freshly ground pepper, nutmeg
- 1 bunch chervil

Peel, wash and dice the celeriac. Cook for at least 1 hour in salted boiling water containing the lemon quarters. Check with the point of a sharp knife to confirm when cooking is complete.

Drain and discard the lemon. Add the double cream.

Season with salt, pepper and dust with grated nutmeg. Allow to simmer on a very low heat until the cream has been absorbed by the celeriac.

Transfer to the blender and make into a purée. Check the seasoning and reserve.

In a frying pan, melt the goose fat and gently brown the livers. Season with salt and pepper. Add a sprinkling of balsamic vinegar.

Arrange the livers on individual plates. Add the celeriac purée and decorate with the chervil.

Poulet à la Provençale
Chicken Provençale

Recommended side dish : Ratatouille

Serves 4/5
Preparation : 15 minutes
   Cooking : 40 minutes

- 1 free-range chicken weighing about 1.4kg (3lb)
- 1 large onion – sliced
- 4 cloves garlic – sliced
- 25cl (9fl oz) chicken stock
- 3 tablespoons tomato purée
- olive oil
- salt, freshly ground pepper, cayenne, Herbes de Provence

Cut the chicken into 8 pieces and arrange in an oven dish with the skin uppermost. Brush with olive oil. Season with salt, pepper and cayenne.

Cook under the grill for about 30 minutes. The skin should crisp slowly without getting charred. Therefore care should be taken not to get too close to the grill.

In a casserole, brown the onions and the garlic in the olive oil. Pour over the stock and add the purée. Stir well. Season with salt and pepper.

Coat the pieces of chicken with the tomato sauce and sprinkle with some Herbes de Provence. Place the chicken in the casserole and put in the oven (Mk. ½ – 130°C) for 5 or 10 minutes.

Serve in the casserole or in a warm serving dish.

Poulet aux Pommes et Crème de Cidre
Chicken with Apples and Cider Cream

Serves 5
Preparation : 20 minutes
   Cooking : 1 hr 40 minutes

- 1 free-range chicken weighing about 1.4kg (3lb)
- 1kg apples
- 20cl (7fl oz) dry cider
- 1 chicken stock cube
- 20cl (7fl oz) double cream
- 2 teaspoons cinnamon
- goose fat
- salt, freshly ground pepper, cayenne

Brush the chicken with a tablespoon of goose fat. Season with salt, pepper and cayenne and place in a pre-heated oven (Mk.7 – 220°C).

Peel the apples and cut into pieces. Cook in the frying pan with goose fat, stirring regularly. Season liberally with salt, pepper and cinnamon. Reserve.

To make the Cream of Cider sauce, boil the cider in a pan and reduce by three quarters. Add the chicken stock cube and dissolve well. Then add the double cream. Bring to the boil and turn off the heat. Correct the seasoning if necessary. In the last quarter of an hour, arrange the apples around the chicken.

When ready, cut up the chicken, coat with the reheated cream of cider and serve with the cinnamon apples.

Coquelets aux Cèpes
Chicken with Cep Mushrooms

Serves 4
Preparation : 20 minutes
    Cooking : 45 minutes

- 2 young chickens between 600 to 800g each
  (1¼ to 1¾lb each)
- 8 nice, fresh cep mushrooms
- juice of 1 lemon
- 1 tablespoon freshly chopped parsley
- olive oil
- salt, freshly ground pepper

Clean the ceps and cut into pieces.

Cut the young chickens into eight.

Heat the olive oil in a casserole. Add the chicken pieces and lightly brown all over, making sure the skin is properly cooked. This should take about 12 minutes or so.

Add the ceps to the casserole and sprinkle with olive oil. Reduce the heat as low as possible, cover the casserole and cook for 30 minutes.

Half-way through cooking, add the salt, pepper and lemon juice.

Serve hot and decorate with the chopped parsley.

Poulet à l'Ail
Chicken with Garlic

Recommended side dishes : Braised fennel
Diced celeriac browned in goose fat

Serves 4
Preparation : 20 minutes
Cooking : 1 hr 20 minutes

- 1 free range chicken weighing about 1.4kg (3lb), with liver
- 4 heads of garlic (about 20 cloves)
- 1 large celery stick
- goose fat
- salt, freshly ground pepper, cayenne

Brown the liver gently in a pan with goose fat.

Crush 5 cloves garlic and cut the celery stick into small pieces.

Mix together in a blender liver, the crushed cloves of garlic, celery pieces and 1 tablespoon of goose fat to make a purée. Season with salt and pepper.

Stuff the chicken with the mixture.

Place the chicken in an ovenware dish. Coat with the goose fat. Season with salt, pepper an cayenne. Put in the oven (Mk.6½ – 210°C) and leave to cook for about 1 hour 15 minutes.

After 20 minutes in the oven, baste the chicken with a glassful of hot salted water. Put the rest of the garlic which has not been peeled, around the chicken and leave to cook until the end.

Poulet Farci à l'Ail
Chicken with Garlic Stuffing

Recommended side dishes : Braised chicory
                          Provençale tomatoes

Serves 5
Preparation : 30 minutes
    Cooking : 2 hrs

- 1 free range chicken weighing about 1.5kg (3¼lb) with liver
  and gizzards
- 3 garlic heads
- 1 egg + yolk
- salt, freshly ground pepper, cayenne
- goose fat
- Herbes de Provence

Prepare the garlic cloves and cook in a steamer for 30 minutes.

Cut the liver and gizzard into very small pieces. Add a little goose fat to a pan and brown them over a medium heat.

Transfer to the blender. Add the garlic and the eggs. Season with salt, pepper and cayenne.

Stuff the chicken with the coarse mixture and seal the rear end of the carcass with a ball of aluminium foil, or by sewing the opening together.

Brush the chicken with a tablespoon of goose fat. Season with salt and pepper, and dust with Herbes de Provence.

Place in the oven to cook (Mk.7 – 220°C) for 1 hour 15 minutes.

Half way through the cooking, pour a glassful of hot salted water into the roasting tin and baste the chicken with the cooking juices.

Cut up the chicken and slice the stuffing.

Deglaze the tin with hot water and serve the gravy separately.

LE PAQUET
10,00 FF

Bourguignon de Magret de Canard
Duck Breast Casserole

This dish can be prepared in advance. When the sauce has reached room temperature, the meat may be added and then reheated over a gentle heat.

Serves 5
Preparation : 25 minutes
   Cooking : 1 hr 10 minutes

- 5 duck breasts
- 3 large onions – sliced thinly
- 4 cloves garlic
- 200g (7oz) tin of mushrooms
- 150g (5oz) pickling onions or shallots – peeled
- 25cl (9fl oz) dry red wine
- 1 bouquet garni
- salt, freshly ground pepper, cayenne
- nutmeg

With a very sharp knife, remove as much fat from the breasts as possible (do not leave more than 1mm – about ¹⁄₁₆in).

In a casserole, melt the fat of two breasts over a low heat. Throw away the part that does not melt and only keep the equivalent of 3 tablespoons of fat.

In this fat, sear the duck breasts for 2 or 3 minutes – they must be crisp outside and pink inside. Season with salt and pepper. Take out the meat and reserve.

Brown the sliced onions in the casserole. Then add the garlic.

Pour in the red wine and add the bouquet garni. Season with salt, pepper, cayenne and freshly grated nutmeg.

Cook uncovered to reduce.

Put 100g (3½oz) of mushrooms in the blender and chop finely. Add the to the casserole together with the remainder of the mushrooms and the small onions.

Boil vigorously for 20 to 30 minutes to reduce the liquid.

When the sauce thickens, remove the bouquet garni and adjust the seasoning.

10 to 15 minutes before serving, return the duck breasts to the casserole. Cover and leave to simmer.

Magrets de Canard en Papillotes
Duck Breasts in their Bags

Recommended side dishes : Celeriac purée
Parsley mushrooms
Provençale tomatoes

Serves 4
Preparation : 15 minutes
Cooking : 15 minutes

- 4 duck breasts
- 20cl (7fl oz) crèmethe
- 2 tablespoons strong mustard
- salt, freshly ground pepper, cayenne, Herbes de Provence

Place each breast fatty side downwards in the middle of a rectangle of aluminium foil. Season with salt, pepper, cayenne and some Herbes de Provence. Draw the long edges of the foil together and close the bag by folding over a couple of times. Pinch the ends together and pull upwards to form a gondola.

Cook over the barbecue or grill, in an open fire or in a preheated oven (Mk.10 – 250°C). Cook for 5 to 10 minutes, depending on the method of cooking and the heat applied. If in doubt, partially open one of the bags after 6 minutes to see how things are doing.

When ready, carve the breasts into thin slices and keep warm, retaining 2 tablespoons of the cooking liquid to make the sauce.

Mix the liquid with the mustard and crème the, pour over the duck slices and serve immediately.

Magret aux Olives
Duck Breast with Olives

Recommended side dishes : Parsley mushrooms
Aubergine gratin
Courgette gratin

Serves 4
Preparation : 15 minutes
Cooking : 20 minutes

- 500g (1lb) green olives – stoned
- 4 duck breasts
- salt, freshly ground pepper, cayenne
- olive oil

Purée 200g (7oz) olives in the blender with 1 tablespoon of olive oil.

Remove three-quarters of the fat covering the breasts. Use a third of the fat. Cut into cubes and melt slowly over a low heat. Discard the residue.

Add the olive purée. Season with salt and pepper, then add the rest of the olives and cook for 5 minutes.

For pink centres, fry the breasts in a non-stick pan for 6 minutes each side, starting with the fatty side. Vary the cooking time according to taste. Turn off the heat.

Cut the breasts into slices 1cm (½in) thick, coat with the olive purée and serve on warm plates.

Magrets de Canard à l'Orange
Duck Breasts with Orange

Serves 4
Preparation : 20 minutes
    Cooking : 15 minutes

- 4 duck breasts
- 3 oranges
- juice of 2 oranges
- zest of 1 orange
- salt and freshly ground pepper

Using a very sharp knife, remove the fat from the duck breasts, leaving a thin film on the meat which is barely visible.

Dice the fat from one duck very finely. Discard the remainder.

In a casserole, melt the diced fat over a low heat.

Remove any residue with a slotted spoon.

Peel the oranges and cut into slices. Fry gently for 3 minutes in the ducks fat.

In an ovenware dish, arrange the breasts fatty side uppermost. Season with salt.

Spread the orange slices and zest around the duck, adding the juice of another 2 oranges.

Place under a pre-heated grill (10cm – 4in) for 6 minutes.

Transfer to a board and carve slices about 0.5cm (¼in) thick. Then, unless the breasts are preferred very pink, replace in the cooking dish and put in the oven (Mk.¼ – 100°C) for a further 2 or 3 minutes. Serve immediately.

Canard aux Olives
Duck with Olives

Serves 4   (Phase 2)
Preparation : 20 minutes
   Cooking : 2 hrs 10 minutes

- 1 large duck with the liver
- 300g (11oz) green olives – stoned
- 300g (11oz) black olives – stoned
- 2 eggs
- 2 slices wholemeal bread
- 10cl (4fl oz) double cream
- 1 onion – peeled
- salt, freshly ground pepper, cayenne
- olive oil

Cut up the liver and brown quickly in some olive oil.

Soak the bread in the double cream and allow to swell.

Use the liquidizer to make a paste of the liver, a third of the green and black olives, the eggs and the bread soaked in cream. Season with salt, Herbes de Provence, pepper and cayenne.

Stuff the duck with this mixture and seal the body cavity with an onion.

Put the duck in a roasting tin. Sprinkle salt, pepper and cayenne over the top and place in the oven (Mk.2½ – 160°C).

After an hour, slowly pour a glass of salted water over the duck and then add the rest of the olives to the contents of the tin and stir together.

Return the duck to the oven and continue cooking at a reduced temperature (Mk. ½ – 130°C) for another hour.

Remove the olives with a slotted spoon and reserve in a warm place. Skim-off some of the fat in the tin and deglaze the remainder with a glassful of boiling water.

Carve the duck in the roasting tin, to conserve the juices. Arrange the pieces on a warm dish.

Finish deglazing the roasting tin and reheat the sauce before pouring into a warm sauceboat.

Filets de Dindonneau au Porto
Fillets of Turkey with Port

Serves 4   (Phase 2)
Preparation : 20 minutes
    Cooking : 30 minutes

- 4 turkey fillets
- 4 leek whites
- 2 shallots – chopped
- 20cl (7fl oz) chicken stock
- 20cl (7fl oz) double cream
- 2 tablespoons port
- salt, pepper, cayenne
- olive oil

Cut the leek whites into thin rings and fry them gently with the shallots in some olive oil in a casserole.

Add the chicken stock, double cream, port, salt, pepper and cayenne. Cover and leave to cook on a low heat for 10 minutes.

Put the turkey fillets into the casserole a leave to cook over a medium heat for 10 minutes. Remove, arrange on a serving dish and reserve in a warm place.

Strain the leek whites in a colander and reserve the sauce. Purée the leeks and arrange around the meat on the serving dish.

Reduce the sauce till creamy. Pour over the meat and serve.

Pintade Flambée aux Endives
Flambé of Guinea Fowl with Chicory

Serves 4
Preparation : 25 minutes
   Cooking : 55 minutes

- 1 guinea fowl weighing 1.2kg (2½lb)
- 8 chicories
- goose fat
- ½ glass brandy
- 10cl (4fl oz) double cream
- salt, freshly ground pepper, cayenne

Coat the guinea fowl with goose fat. Season with salt, pepper and cayenne.

Put in an ovenware dish and roast in the oven (Mk.8 – 230°C) for 55 minutes.

During this time, boil the chicory for 30 minutes in a pan of salted water. Drain well.

A quarter of an hour before the guinea fowl is cooked, add the chicory to the dish in the oven.

When the guinea fowl is done, remove from the oven. Take out the chicory and put on a serving dish.

Cut the guinea fowl into pieces in the oven dish and flambé with the brandy. Arrange the pieces of fowl on the serving dish with the chicory.

Deglaze the oven dish with the double cream and pour the sauce into a warm boat.

Perdrix en Papillote
Partridge in a Bag

Recommended side dishes : Broccoli
French beans

Serves 4
Preparation : 20 minutes
Cooking : 30 minutes

- 4 partridges – cleaned and plucked
- 4 tablespoons goose fat
- aluminium foil
- 1 box of watercress
- salt, freshly ground pepper

Halve the partridges down their length.

Coat with goose fat. Season with salt and pepper.

Place each half on a foil sheet, which should be folded over at the edges to form a bag.

Place the aluminium bags in a pre-heated oven (Mk.6½ – 210°C) and cook for
30 minutes.

Serve the partridge on plates decorated with watercress.

Perdrix au Chou
Partridge with Cabbage

Serves 4
Preparation : 30 minutes
    Cooking : 2 hrs

- 2 partridges
- 2 slices fat bacon
- 1 firm savoy cabbage
- 250g (9oz) diced streaky bacon
- 1 onion
- 1 bouquet garni
- 20cl (7fl oz) chicken stock
- 2 tablespoons goose fat
- salt, pepper

Tie the fat slices over the partridge breasts.

In a large pan, bring 1.5 litres (3lb) of salted water to the boil.

Remove the outer leaves of the cabbage and cut the heart into four quarters.

Blanche for 10 minutes in the boiling water. Drain.

In a large casserole melt the goose fat. Cook the quartered onion and diced streaky bacon for a few minutes, until golden. Remove with a slotted spoon and keep warm.

In the same casserole, cook the partridges over a medium heat for 15 minutes until brown all over. Season with salt and pepper.

Remove the partridges and replace with the cabbage. Season with salt, pepper and add the bouquet garni. Add a little bouillon and allow to simmer for about 15 minutes.

Remove the cabbage and throw away the bouquet garni.

Spread out half the cabbage on a large ovenware dish. Place the partridges on top with the diced streaky bacon. Cover with the remainder of the cabbage and pour the cooking juices over the top. Cover with a sheet of foil and cook in a very hot oven (Mk.8 – 230°C) for about 1 hour.

Faisan à la Choucroute
Pheasant with Sauerkraut

Serves 4
Preparation : 30 minutes
   Cooking : 1 hr 45 minutes

- 2 small pheasants, plucked and cleaned
- 2 broad slices of fat bacon
- 1.2kg (2½lb) raw sauerkraut
- 300g diced streaky bacon
- 2 small onions
- 1 bouquet garni
- juniper berries
- peppercorns
- goose fat
- dry white wine
- ½ glass brandy
- salt and freshly ground pepper

Wash the sauerkraut. Press and drain well.

In a casserole, brown the diced streaky bacon with the quartered onions.

Add the bouquet garni, a dozen juniper berries and some peppercorns.

Then add the sauerkraut. Pour in enough wine to cover the sauerkraut. Bring to the boil, then cover and put the casserole in the oven (Mk. ½ – 130°C) for about an hour

Tie the bacon fat onto the breast of each pheasant. Season all over with salt and pepper.

In a second casserole, heat 2 tablespoons of goose fat. Brown the pheasants all over and when golden brown, cover and continue cooking on a gentle heat for 30 minutes.

Remove the sauerkraut from the oven to see whether it is cooked – it should be translucent. Drain and discard the onion and bouquet garni. Arrange on the serving dish and reserve in a warm place.

Cut the pheasants in half and flambé with the brandy.

Remove the string and place the pheasants on the bed of sauerkraut. Deglaze the casserole in which the pheasants were cooked with a little of the white wine and pour this over the dish or into the sauceboat.

Serve immediately.

Pigeons aux Petits Pois
Pigeons with Garden Peas

Serves 4
Preparation : 20 minutes
   Cooking : 55 minutes

- 4 pigeons – plucked and cleaned
- 2 onions – sliced
- 15cl (5fl oz) dry white wine
- 15cl (5fl oz) chicken stock
- 500g (1lb) petits pois
- 125g (4oz) cured ham – in slices about ½cm (¼in) thick
- 2 tablespoons goose fat
- salt, freshly ground pepper, cayenne

Cut the ham into small cubes.

Season the inside of the carcasses with salt, pepper and cayenne.

Melt the goose fat in a large casserole. Put in the onions and brown gently for 2 or 3 minutes. Add the pigeons and cook until golden all over.

Pour in the white wine and add the ham. Cook over a low heat for 10 minutes.

Add the chicken stock and cover. Leave to cook over a very gentle heat for 20 minutes.

Add the petits pois and simmer for another 15 minutes.

Serve in a deep dish together with all the cooking juices.

Pigeonneaux Farcis au Thym
Pigeon with Thyme Stuffing

Recommended side dish : Sweet pepper purée

Serves 4
Preparation : 20 minutes
    Cooling : 45 minutes

- 4 young pigeons
- 4 shallots – sliced
- 8 cloves garlic – sliced
- 1 large bunch fresh thyme
- 1 bunch parsley
- ½ glass brandy
- goose fat
- salt, freshly ground pepper

Have the pigeons plucked and cleaned, and the lower leg and neck removed. Ask for the livers, gizzards and hearts. If not available, buy 200g (7oz) of chicken liver instead.

Cut the livers, gizzards and hearts into small pieces and cook in a little goose fat. Salt and pepper.

In the same pan, brown the shallots and garlic – adding a little goose fat if necessary.

Blend the livers, gizzards, hearts, garlic, shallots with their cooking juices, as well as the thyme and the parsley, to make the stuffing.

Divide the mixture equally between the four pigeons and stuff.

Brush the four birds with goose fat. Season with salt and pepper. Then cook in a pre-heated oven (Mk.5 – 190°C) for 30 to 35 minutes.

Half-way through the cooking, baste with a small glassful of hot salty water.

When cooked, remove the pigeons from the oven and cut in two on a board. Put them back in the cooking tin and flambé with brandy.

Serve at once.

Rôti de Magret
Roast Breast of Duck

Recommended side dishes : Small broad beans
Parsley mushrooms
Cep mushrooms

Serves 4
Preparation : 20 minutes
Cooking : 25 minutes

- 3 duck's breasts
- 2 cloves garlic – peeled
- salt, freshly ground pepper, Herbes de Provence

Remove all the fat from one of the three breasts, by pulling the fat with one hand and cutting the securing membrane with the tip of a sharp knife in the other. Season all three breasts with salt, pepper and herbs.

Then make up the roast by sandwiching the stripped breast between the other two, leaving their fatty parts facing outwards. Tie together with string to secure.

Halve the garlic cloves and insert into the meat by making a deep and narrow slit with the point of a sharp knife.

Put the duck breasts in a tin and place in the oven (Mk.7 – 220°C). Cook for 25 minutes. After 15, remove as much fat as possible from the bottom of the tin. Then pour half a glass of hot salted water over the roast.

When cooked, take the duck out of the oven and slice like rolled beef. Like beef, the centre should be hot and very pink. Serve with the cooking juices and carving juices mixed together.

Variation: The cooking tin can also be deglazed with whipping cream, seasoned with salt, pepper and a pinch of cayenne.

Foie Gras Poêlé aux Champignons Persillés
Sauté of Foie Gras and Parsley Mushrooms

Ideally this dish should be made with fresh foie gras.

Serves 4
Preparation : 20 minutes
   Cooking : 20 minutes

- 500g (1lb 2oz) foie gras
- 600g (1¼lb) button mushrooms
- 5 cloves garlic – crushed
- 3 tablespoons chopped parsley
- 4 tablespoons sherry vinegar
- salt, freshly ground pepper

Clean and slice the mushrooms.

In a large frying pan, heat the oil and sautée the mushrooms. Season with salt and pepper.

When the mushrooms have reduced, discard the cooking juices. Replace with fresh olive oil.

On one side of the frying pan, fry the garlic and parsley over a low heat. Stir into the mushrooms. Reserve and keep warm.

Cut the foie gras down its length into slices 2cm (1in) thick and cook over a low heat in a non-stick pan for about 1 minute on each side. Season with salt and pepper. Remove and reserve on very hot plates.

Discard about half of the fat released by the foie gras. Deglaze the frying pan with the sherry vinegar. Add the mushrooms. Mix well and serve with the foie gras.

Oie Farcie aux Marrons
Stuffed Goose with Chestnuts

Serves 10
Preparation : 30 minutes
   Cooking : 3 hrs 45 minutes

- 1 goose weighing 3kg (6½lb) – with liver if possible
- 2kg (4½lb) fresh chestnuts
- 1 litre (2 pints) chicken stock
- 3 tablespoons of crèmethe
- 2 bay leaves
- 40cl (14fl oz) double cream
- salt, freshly ground pepper, chilli pepper
- Herbes de Provence

Add the bay leaves to the chicken stock and bring to the boil. Add the peeled chestnuts and simmer for 35 minutes. Drain and reserve.

Brown the goose liver in a pan with some goose fat. Salt, pepper and add some Herbes de Provence. (If you cannot come by the goose liver, substitute with 500g (18oz) chicken livers and cook the same way).

Blend together the liver, slightly less than half the chestnuts and the crème the into a coarse paste. Adjust the seasoning, making sure there is enough ground pepper and chilli pepper.

Fill the goose with this stuffing and secure by sewing up the rear opening.

Put the goose in a large tin and place in the oven. Cook in a warm oven (Mk.2½ – 160°C) for at least 3 hours.

While the goose is cooking, remove the dripping which should be stored for future use.

In the last half hour, add the remainder of the chestnuts.

When cooking is completed, remove most of the fat from the pan and deglaze with the whipping cream. Pour the sauce into a boat to accompany the goose.

Escalopes de Dinde à la Crème
Turkey Escalopes with Cream

Recommended side dishes : Spinach
                          French beans

(Phase 2)

Serves 4
Preparation : 10 minutes
   Cooking : 20 minutes

- 4 good slices of turkey breast
- 10cl (4fl oz) dry white wine
- 1 small yoghurt
- 1 tablespoon mustard
- goose fat
- 1 tablespoon freshly chopped parsley

Fry the turkey slices in the goose fat over a medium heat till golden brown.

Season with salt and pepper. Reserve and keep warm on the serving dish.

Deglaze the pan with the white wine. Boil down slightly, then add the yoghurt mixed with the mustard. Stir over a gentle heat.

Coat the escalopes with the sauce and sprinkle with parsley.

Pot-au-Feu de Dinde
Turkey Pot-au-Feu

Serves 6
Preparation : 15 minutes
   Cooking : 1 hr 20 minutes

- 6 turkey thighs
- 3 large onions – sliced
- 1 small celeriac
- 250g (9oz) French beans
- 40cl (14fl oz) chicken stock
- 3 tablespoon goose fat
- bouquet garni
- salt, freshly ground pepper

Put the goose fat in a casserole and brown the sliced onions for a few minutes over a gentle heat.

Meanwhile, cut the celeriac into cubes and cut the french beans into short lengths. Put them in the casserole and mix with the onions. Continue cooking for several minutes.

Arrange the pieces of turkey next to each other on top of the vegetables. Season with salt, pepper and add the bouquet garni. Pour the chicken stock over the top. Raise the heat and bring to the boil. Cover and leave to simmer for 1 hour.

Serve when cooked. Alternatively, allow to get cold so that the fat can be removed easily. Reheat when required.

Dinde aux Pommes
Turkey with Apples

Serves 8
Preparation : 30 minutes
   Cooking : 2 hrs 40 minutes

- 1 turkey weighing 3.5kg (8lb)
- 600g (1¼lb) sliced onions
- 1.5kg (3¼lb) apples (cox)
- 4 cloves garlic – chopped
- 6 leaves fresh sage
- goose fat
- olive oil
- 1 lemon
- salt, freshly ground pepper, cayenne
- 1 glass cider
- 20cl (7fl oz) double cream

In a frying pan brown the onions in olive oil. Add the garlic towards the end.

Peel and quarter the apples. Squeeze lemon over them to prevent them turning brown. Cook one third of the apples in the goose fat over a low heat.

Chop the sage and add to the onions, garlic and apples to make a stuffing. Season with salt, pepper and cayenne.

Stuff the turkey and sew up the opening. Coat the turkey with the goose fat. Season with salt, pepper and sprinkle lightly with cayenne.

Put in a roasting tin, adding a good glass of water and place in a fairly hot oven (Mk.5 – 190°C). Cook for 2 hours and 15 minutes, basting every 30 minutes.

During the last half-hour, pour off the cooking juices and add the rest of the peeled and quartered apples. Pour a quarter of the cooking juices carefully over the apples, reserving the rest to make the sauce.

When the turkey is done, deglaze the roasting tin with the cider, stirring in the reserved juices together with the double cream.

FISH

Morue à la Provençale
Cod Provençale

Recommended side dishes : Leeks
                                          French beans

Serves 4
Preparation : 10 minutes
   Cooking : 50 minutes

- 600g (1¼lb) salted cod
- 4 shallots – sliced
- 25cl (9fl oz) dry white wine
- 25cl (9fl oz) fish stock
- 2 tablespoons tomato paste
- 1 sprig thyme
- 1 tablespoon freshly chopped parsley
- 1 tablespoon freshly chopped basil
- 150g (5oz) green olives – stoned
- 2 bay leaves
- salt, freshly ground pepper

Immerse the fish in water for 24 hours to remove salt, changing the water every 6 hours.

In a deep frying pan or wok, brown the shallots and garlic in olive oil. Stir in the tomato paste. Add the wine, fish stock, thyme, parsley, basil and bay leaves. Bring to the boil and then cook over a gentle heat for 20 minutes.

Drain the fish and cut into 4 pieces. Cook over a low heat in a non-stick pan with olive oil.

When the sauce has reduced to a half, adjust the seasoning.

Reheat the cod by cooking in the sauce for a few minutes.

Serve very hot.

Filets de Sole à la Crème de Soja
Fillets of Sole with Cream of Soya Sauce

Recommended side dishes : Spinach
French beans

Serves 4
Preparation : 20 minutes
Cooking : 20 minutes

- 4 large fillets of sole
- juice of 1 lemon
- 150g (5oz) button mushrooms, washed and sliced
- 20cl (7fl oz) soya cream
- 100g (4oz) peeled prawns
- 1 egg yolk
- olive oil
- salt, freshly ground pepper
- 1 tablespoon fresh parsley

Wash the filets under the tap and pat dry with absorbent kitchen paper.

Heat 2 tablespoons of olive oil in a non-stick frying pan, and gently fry the fish. Pour lemon juice over the top. Season with salt and pepper. Continue cooking over a low heat for 2 minutes. Set aside and keep warm.

Fry the mushrooms over a gentle heat in 2 tablespoons of olive oil.

Discard the cooking juices and the water from the mushrooms. Add the cream of soya, mixed beforehand in a bowl with the egg yolk. Season with salt and pepper. Add the prawns.

Continue cooking over a low heat for a few minutes, stirring continuously.

Arrange the fish on warmed plates and coat with the sauce.

Filets de Sole au Saumon
Fillets of Sole with Salmon

Recommended side dishes : Broccoli
                          Spinach
                          French beans

Serves 4
Preparation : 15 minutes
   Cooking : 20 minutes

- 4 good sized soles
- 300g (10oz) fillet of salmon
- 5 shallots – sliced
- 3 tablespoons crème fraîche
- 15cl (5fl oz) dry white wine
- juice of ½ lemon
- 1 tablespoon freshly chopped parsley

Ask the fishmonger to fillet the sole and then to slice the salmon fillets thinly as for smoked salmon.

Take a fillet of sole and cover with a fillet of salmon and roll the two together. Secure by spiking with a wooden toothpick.

In a pan, brown the shallots a few minutes in olive oil. Then add the white wine. Season with salt and pepper and cook for 1 minute.

Put the fish rolls in an ovenware dish. Season with salt and pepper. Pour the wine mixture over the top.

Place in a fairly hot oven (Mk.5 – 190°C) for 12 to 15 minutes.

Take out of the oven and arrange the fish on a serving dish. Reserve in warm place.

Quickly add the crème fraîche and the lemon juice to the cooking juices in the ovenware dish and blend with a fork.

Coat the fish rolls with the sauce and decorate with parsley before serving.

Nage de Poissons et Fruits de Mer
Fish Soup with Shellfish

Serves 5/6
Preparation : 30 minutes
   Cooking : 40 minutes

- 2kg (4½lb) assorted fish (monkfish, conger eel, bream, hake, mullet, cod . . .)
- 12 langoustines, tiger prawns or giant scampi – uncooked
- 1 litre (2 pints) mussels
- 4 white leeks
- 1 stick of celery with leaves removed
- 1 onion
- 3 shallots
- 3 cloves garlic
- 1 bouquet garni
- 3 tablespoons of crème fraîche
- olive oil
- sea salt, peppercorns, cayenne

Have the fish cleaned, de-scaled and trimmed by the fishmonger. Cut into sections (very large slices).

Clean the mussels in several changes of water. Remove the beards and throw away any broken shells. Then, leaving them in a very large pan of clean water, throw away those that rise to the surface or do no close.

Peel, wash and chop finely the celery, leeks, onion, shallots and garlic.

In a large casserole, heat 3 tablespoons of olive oil and sweat the vegetables for 5 minutes.

Add 1.5 litres (3 pints) water, the bouquet garni, salt, peppercorns and 3 good pinches of cayenne. Simmer the soup for 15 to 20 minutes with the lid removed.

Add the fish to the soup: first, the fish with solid flesh(monkfish, conger eel) and then about 5 minutes later, the fish with fine grained flesh (hake, cod, bream, mullet...)

Add the mussels and the langoustines 2 minutes later and leave to cook for a further 3 to 5 minutes.

With a slotted spoon, recover the fish and shellfish and keep warm in in a soup tureen.

Remove the bouquet garni from the soup. Adjust the seasoning and add the crème fraîche. Cook for a further 1 or 2 minutes and pour over the fish.

Serve immediately.

Filets de Saumon Grillés au Tamari
Grilled Salmon Fillets with Tamari

Recommended side dish : Leeks with olive oil dressing

Serves 4
Preparation : 10 minutes
   Cooking : 10 minutes

- 800g (1¾lb) salmon fillets
- 1 lemon
- olive oil
- tamari (thick soy sauce)
- fine sea salt
- pepper, Herbes de Provence

Cut the fillets into 4 equal pieces. Brush with olive oil. Season with salt and pepper.

Pre-heat the oven grill.

Place the fillet pieces in an ovenware dish with the skin facing uppermost. Sprinkle lightly with Herbes de Provence.

Cook under the grill for 10 minutes.

Meanwhile, prepare the sauce: ⅓ lemon juice, ⅓ olive oil, ⅓ tamari, a pinch of sea salt and a pinch of pepper.

Arrange the salmon on the plates, with the skin side down. Sprinkle with parsley. Stir the sauce well, pour over the top and serve.

Loup Grillé au Fenouil et Flambé au Pastis
Grilled Sea Bass with Fennel Flamed with Pastis

Recommended side dishes : Braised fennel
Leeks sautéd in olive oil

Serves 4/5
Preparation : 20 minutes
Cooking : 40 minutes

- 1 sea bass weighing 1.5 to 2kg (3½ to 4½lb)
- fennel stalks
- olive oil
- 3 cloves garlic – crushed
- ½ glass pastis (Pernod)
- salt, freshly ground pepper, cayenne
- 3 lemons

Have the fish cleaned and de-scaled by your fishmonger.

Make a marinade with the olive oil, crushed garlic, salt, pepper and cayenne. Brush liberally in the body cavity and fill completely with fennel stalks.

Place some fennel stalks on the bottom a roasting tin and lay the fish on top. Brush the the sea bass liberally with the marinade.

Put the fish under the grill for 15 to 20 minutes. Allow to char. Turn, brush with the marinade again and cook for a further 15 or 20 minutes

Transfer the fish to a serving dish and remove the fennel stalks.

Flambé with the pastis.

Fillet and arrange on a serving dish.

If desired, the fish may be served with a dressing of olive oil, lemon juice, salt and pepper.

Note: This is an ideal recipe for a barbecue. Be careful however, not to overcook the fish and be prepared to use aluminium foil to prevent the flesh getting dry and fibrous.

Merlu Paysanne
Hake Country Style

Serves 4/5
Preparation : 20 minutes
   Cooking : 1 hr 10 minutes

- 1 hake weighing about 1.5kg (3¼lb)
- 1kg fresh petits pois (or frozen)
- 2 small celeriac
- 10 silverskin onions
- 500g (1lb) asparagus tips
- 4 cloves garlic – sliced
- olive oil
- salt, freshly ground pepper, cayenne

Ask the fishmonger to clean the hake and cut it into slices 2.5cm (1in) thick.

Prepare the vegetables. Ideally, steam the asparagus and the petit pois in a two-tiered steamer. Alternatively, cook in boiling water.

Cook the celeriac and silverskin onions for 30 to 40 minutes in a small amount of water with olive oil and salt.

In a small pan, brown the sliced garlic in 2 tablespoons of olive oil.

Pour garlic and oil into an ovenware dish. Add the slices of hake and lay flat. Season with salt, pepper and cayenne. Place about 10cm (40in) below the grill and cook for 5 to 10 minutes.

Arrange the petits pois, asparagus, celeriac and onions in a terracotta dish, and then add the slices of hake. Trickle fresh olive oil on the top and serve.

Limandes à la Crétoise
Lemon Sole Cretan Style

Recommended side dish : Brussels sprouts

Serves 4
Preparation : 10 minutes
   Cooking : 10 minutes

- 6 lemon sole fillets
- 3 onions – sliced
- 3 lemons
- 4 bay leaves
- 2 sprigs thyme
- 1 glass olive oil
- salt, freshly ground pepper

Prepare a marinade with the olive oil, sliced onions, lemon juice, thyme, bay leaf, salt and pepper.

Marinade the fish fillets for 20 minutes.

Then pour the marinade in a frying pan over a medium heat. When the marinade is hot, add the fillets and poach for 5 minutes each side.

Serve with a dressing of olive oil and lemon juice according to taste.

Lotte à l'Américaine
Monkfish American Style

Serves 4
Preparation : 20 minutes
   Cooking : 40 minutes

- 1.5kg (3½lb) boned monkfish
- 50cl (18fl oz) dry white wine
- 2 tablespoons tomato paste
- 4 shallots – sliced
- 2 garlic cloves – sliced
- 100g crushed tomatoes (tinned)
- olive oil
- salt, freshly ground pepper
- 5cl (2fl oz) brandy

Cut the monkfish into short lengths of 5 to 6cm (2in) and in a non-stick pan, brown in olive oil over a low heat.

Season with salt, pepper and flambé with the brandy.

Deglaze the pan with a tablespoon of dry white wine. Reserve and keep warm.

In a deep frying pan or wok, soften the sliced shallots and garlic with 2 tablespoons of olive oil. Add the tomato paste and simmer for a few minutes, stirring frequently.

Add the rest of the white wine. Season with salt and pepper.

Cover and bring to the boil. Remove the lid and simmer for 10 minutes

Add the drained tomato pieces and finally the fish. Bring back to the boil and serve immediately.

Soles Normandes
Normandy Sole

Recommended side dishes : Spinach
French beans

Serves 4
Preparation : 15 minutes
Cooking : 20 minutes

- 6 large fillets of sole
- 50cl (1 pint) milk
- 100g (4oz) peeled prawns
- 200g (7oz) tinned button mushrooms
- 1 egg yolk
- 20cl (7fl oz) crème fraîche
- 1 lemon
- salt, pepper

Poach the fillets in milk and simmer very gently for 10 minutes. Drain, reserve and keep warm.

In a pan, mix the prawns, drained buttons mushrooms, crème fraîche and lemon juice. Warm through over a gentle heat for 5 minutes.

Away from the heat, add the egg yolk, stirring vigorously. Season very sparingly with pepper and salt, then pour over the fillets of sole and serve immediately.

Poulpe aux Oignons
Octopus with Onions

Serves 5
Preparation : 15 minutes
    Cooking : 2 hrs 10 minutes

- 1kg (2¼lb) prepared octopus
- 500g (1lb) silverskin onions – skinned
- 5 big tomatoes
- 3 tablespoons sherry vinegar
- 4 cloves garlic – crushed
- 2 bay leaves
- 1 glass dry white wine
- 3 pinches cinnamon

Place the octopus in a casserole of water and cook for 30 minutes.

Drain and cut into small pieces.

Pour boiling water on the tomatoes. Then peel, halve and remove the seeds. Cut the flesh into large cubes.

Warm 3 tablespoons of olive oil in a casserole and brown the chopped octopus for 10 minutes. Add the garlic and cook a further 1 or 2 minutes, stirring well.

Then put in the vinegar, tomatoes, bay leaves, white wine, salt, pepper and cinnamon. Cook over a gentle heat for 30 minutes. Add the onions, cover and leave to cook for a good hour.

Rougets à l'Anis
Red Mullet with Aniseed

Serves 4
Preparation : 15 minutes
    Cooking : 20 minutes

- 4 red mullet, cleaned, de-scaled and pared
- 400g (14oz) fennel
- 1 teaspoon aniseed grains
- olive oil
- salt, freshly ground pepper

Clean the fennel and cut into strips. Blanch in boiling salted water for 6 minutes. Drain well.

In an ovenproof dish, make a bed of fennel using half the strips. Place the fish on top. Cover with the remainder of the fennel. Sprinkle the aniseed grains over the dish. Sprinkle with olive oil. Season with salt and pepper.

Place in a very hot oven (Mk.10 – 250°C) for about 12 minutes.

Serve in the ovenproof dish.

Rougets à la Menthe Fraîche
Red Mullet with a Fresh Mint sauce

Recommended side dishes: Braised chicory
                         Broccoli purée

Serves 4
Preparation : 15 minutes
   Cooking : 15 minutes

- 8 red mullet cleaned and de-scaled
- 100g (4oz) freshly chopped mint
- 6 cloves garlic
- 5cl (2fl oz) old wine vinegar
- 5cl (2fl oz) balsamic vinegar
- 3 tablespoons olive oil
- salt, freshly ground pepper

Pre-heat the oven to a very cool 65°C.

Take a non-stick pan, add 2 tablespoons olive oil and cook the red mullet 4 minutes each side. Season with salt and pepper during the cooking.

Reserve and keep warm in the oven.

Slice the garlic very finely.

Pour the two vinegars and 1 tablespoon olive oil into a pan. Add the garlic and chopped mint. Season lightly with salt and pepper.

Bring to the boil and stir for 4 to 5 minutes.

Remove the red mullet from the oven, pour the sauce over the fish and serve.

Filets de Rouget à la Crème
Red Mullet with a wine and Cream Sauce

Recommended side dishes : Leeks sautéd in olive oil
French bean purée

Serves 4
Preparation : 20 minutes
Cooking : 20 minutes

- 8 nice red mullet fillets
- juice of 1 lemon
- 3 shallots – sliced
- 1 glass dry white wine
- 20cl (7fl oz) crème fraîche
- sea salt, freshly ground pepper
- olive oil
- 1 tablespoon freshly chopped parsley

Fry the shallots in olive oil over a low heat. When they are well softened without caramelising, add the white wine. Raise the temperature to reduce the liquid by half. Season with salt and pepper. Reserve.

Wash the fillets under the tap. Pat them dry with absorbent kitchen paper and then lay flat in a large dish. Squeeze out the lemon over the fish.

Preheat 2 tablespoons of olive oil in a non-stick frying pan over a very low heat.

Cook the fillets on both sides. Season with salt and pepper.

Meanwhile, add the crème fraîche to the reserved onion mixture. Heat over a gentle heat and allow to thicken, stirring regularly.

Arrange the fillets on individual plates and coat with the sauce. Sprinkle with parsley and serve.

Saumon en Croûte de Sel
Salmon in a Salt Crust

Recommended side dishes : Chicory with soya cream
　　　　　　　　　　　　　Leeks
　　　　　　　　　　　　　Broccoli

Serves 4
Preparation : 10 minutes
　Cooking : 40 minutes

- 1 really fresh salmon weighing 1.2kg (2½lb)
- 2kg (4½lb) coarse sea salt
- juice of 3 lemons
- 10cl (4fl oz) olive oil
- salt, freshly ground pepper

Have the salmon cleaned and de-scaled by the fishmonger, but leave the head on.

On an oven tray or ovenproof dish large enough to accommodate the fish, lay a thin bed of salt. Place the fish on top and cover entirely with salt to a depth of at least 1cm (½ in).

Pre-heat the oven (Mk.10 – 250°C) and cook for 40 minutes.

When ready, break the crust gently and lift off together with the skin, using a large broad knife.

Make a dressing by mixing the olive oil, lemon, salt and pepper. Pour the dressing over the fish and serve.

Filets de Bar à la Sauce d'Echalotes
Sea Bass Fillets with Shallot Sauce

Recommended side dishes : Broccoli
                                     Spinach
                                     Cauliflower

Serves 4
Preparation : 20 minutes
  Cooking : 5 minutes

- 1 kg (2¼lb) sea bass fillets
- 4 shallots
- 2 tablespoons olive oil
- 20 cl (7fl oz) double cream
- For the fish stock: use the head and bones
- 1 onion
- 1 stick of celery
- 2 sprigs parsley
- 1 bouquet garni
- ½ glass dry white wine
- ½ glass red wine vinegar
- salt, pepper

Ask the fishmonger to prepare the fillets and reserve the head and bones for making the fish stock.

To prepare the fish stock, chop up the onion, celery and parsley.

Tip into 1.5 litres of water together with the bouquet garni, and boil for 30 minutes. Add the white wine and the vinegar. Allow to cool and pass through a conical strainer.

Add the fish head and bones to the stock. Bring to the boil and continue to reduce over a low heat, until all that remains is a glassful. Season with salt and pepper.

Liquidize the shallots and mix with the olive oil.

In an ovenware dish that has been lightly oiled, place the filets with the skin side downwards. Season with salt and pepper. Spread the shallot and oil mixture on the fillets.

Place in the oven about 10cm (4in) below the grill, and cook for 6 to 7 minutes.

Mix the glass of fish stock with the double cream. Check seasoning. Cook gently for a further 1 minute.

Coat the fillets with the sauce and serve.

Dorades à la Basquaise
Sea Bream Basque Style

Recommended side dishes : Ratatouille
Provençale tomatoes

Serves 4
Preparation : 20 minutes
   Cooking : 25 minutes

- 2 sea bream weighing about 600 to 700g
  (between 1¼ and 1½lb) each
- 5 cloves garlic – sliced thinly
- ½ glass sherry vinegar
- 2 lemons
- olive oil
- 1 bunch parsley
- salt, freshly ground pepper, cayenne

Ask the fishmonger to scale and clean the bream.

Stuff with parsley and 2 or 3 lemon slices. Season with salt, pepper and cayenne.

Arrange in an ovenware dish, brush with olive oil and place in the oven (Mk.5 – 190°C). Cook for 20 minutes – turning after 10 minutes, to cook the other side.

Fillet the sea bream. Arrange on warm plates. Squeeze lemon juice over the top and reserve in a warm place.

Immediately put the sliced garlic in a pan with 3 tablespoons olive oil. Cook until barely golden. Season with salt, pepper and cayenne. At the last moment, add the sherry vinegar. Pour the boiling sauce over the fish and serve at once.

Calamars à la Provençale
Squid Provençale

Serves 4/5
Preparation : 15 minutes
   Cooking : 45 minutes

- 1.25kg (2½lb) squid
- 400g (14oz) green mild chillis
- 6 ripe tomatoes
- 5 cloves garlic
- olive oil
- salt, freshly ground pepper, cayenne

Ask the fishmonger to prepare the squid, leaving just the body and the tentacles.

Drop the tomatoes in boiling water for 30 seconds before removing the skins. Halve and remove the seeds. Cut the flesh into large cubes and reduce over a very low heat in a casserole containing 2 tablespoons of olive oil. Season with salt and pepper, then reserve.

Fry the green chillies very gently in olive oil for at least 20 minutes. Season with salt and pepper. In the last 5 minutes, add the sliced garlic and cook until pale golden, making certain it does not burn.

Fry the tentacles and body of the squid over a gentle heat in some olive oil. Season with salt, pepper and cayenne.

Turn out the chillis and garlic with their cooking juices into a serving dish. Add the squid and cover with the tomato coulis. Mix well and simmer in the oven for 15 minutes in a very cool oven set at 70°C. Serve on warm plates.

Brochettes d'Espadron
Swordfish on Skewers

Recommended side dishes : Ratatouille
Green salad

Serves 4
Preparation : 20 minutes
Cooking : 15 minutes

- 1kg (2¼lb) of prepared swordfish
- 4 firm tomatoes
- 2 onions
- 4 green peppers
- olive oil
- oregano, salt, freshly ground pepper
- Herbes de Provence

Cut the fish into 2.5cm (1in) cubes.

Quarter the tomatoes and onions.

Cut open the peppers, remove the stalk and seeds and cut into 2 to 3cm (1in) squares.

Load the skewers as follows: pepper, tomato, onion, swordfish, onion tomato....
Arrange on an ovenware dish. Brush with olive oil and sprinkle with Herbes de Provence, salt, freshly ground pepper and oregano.

Place about 10cm (4in) under the grill and cook for about 15 minutes. Turn occasionally and baste regularly with the cooking juices.

Truites aux Amandes
Trout with Almonds

Recommended side dishes : Courgettes with olive oil dressing
Spinach with soya cream

Serves 4
Preparation : 10 minutes
   Cooking : 15 minutes

- 4 plump trout
- 80g (3oz) flaked almonds
- 2 lemons
- 1 tablespoon sherry vinegar
- 2 tablespoons freshly chopped parsley
- olive oil
- salt, freshly ground pepper, Herbes de Provence

Have the trout cleaned by the fishmonger.

Dust the body cavity with Herbes de Provence. Season with salt and pepper.

In a non-stick frying pan, gently heat 4 tablespoons of olive oil.

Place the trout in the pan and cook for 6 minutes on each side. Reserve and keep warm on a serving dish in a very cool oven at 80–100°C.

In another pan, add 1 tablespoon of olive oil and fry the almonds until golden brown. Season with salt and pepper. Add the sherry vinegar.

Pour the vinegar and almond mixture over the trout.

Serve with lemons cut in half.

Tartare de Thon
Tuna Tartare

Serves 4
Preparation : 20 minutes
No cooking

- 1kg (2¼lb) very fresh tuna
- 4 shallots – very finely chopped
- 2 lemons
- 3 tablespoons olive oil
- 1 bunch fresh coriander
- 3 tablespoons freshly chopped parsley
- 1 tablespoon chopped chives
- salt, freshly ground pepper,
- 1 teaspoon cayenne

Prepare the tuna by removing the skin and all the bones.

Cut the flesh into small ½cm (¼in) cubes. Season with salt, pepper and cayenne. Pour olive oil over the top and mix well.

Add the chopped shallots, parsley and chives.

Place in the fridge for 1 or 2 hours.

Serve with a green salad. Before eating, squeeze the juice of 2 lemons over the dish.

Thon en Brandade de Tomate
Tuna, Tomato and Scrambled Egg

Recommended side dishes : Green salad
                          Chicory salad

Serves 4
Preparation : 15 minutes
    Cooking : 45 minutes

- 500g (1lb) tuna in brine
- 500g (1lb) tomato coulis
- 500g (1lb) tomatoes, blanched, skinned, deseeded and diced
- 1 shallot, finely sliced
- 1 clove garlic – crushed
- 1 tablespoon olive oil
- 1 sachet Herbes de Provence
- 3 egg yolks + 1 egg
- 5 cloves garlic – crushed
- 3 tablespoons freshly chopped parsley
- 4 tablespoons olive oil
- 20cl (7fl oz) double cream

Drain the tuna.

Purée the tuna, garlic, parsley and 4 tablespoons olive oil in a food processor. Reserve.

Put the tomato coulis (see below for instructions on how to make a coulis) in a bain-marie with the eggs and cream. Cook, whisking the mixture all the all the time until it thickens.

Add the tuna purée and blend with a spatula.

Pour into an soufflé dish and place in a very cool oven (Mk.½ – 130°C) for 30 to 35 minutes.

Before serving, sprinkle with grated gruyère cheese and place under the grill for a few minutes.

Serve immediately.

To make the coulis:

(add a further 15 to 20 minutes to the overall cooking time, if the coulis is made whilst preparing the dish).

Sauté the shallots and garlic with the olive oil in a pan over a low heat for 4 minutes or until transparent.

Add the tomatoes and sachet of herbes and simmer for 10 to 12 minutes.

Remove the sachet and purée in the mixture in the blender.

Return to the heat, bring to the boil. Adjust seasoning. Simmer for a further 5 minutes.

Thon au Vinaigre d'Ail
Tuna with Garlic Vinegar

Recommended side dishes : Aubergine gratin
Cauliflower

Serves 4
Preparation : 15 minutes
  Cooking : 20 minutes

- 2 thick slices of fresh tuna – weighing about 800g (1¾lb) in all
- 4 cloves garlic – finely sliced
- olive oil
- sherry vinegar
- salt, freshly ground pepper

Heat 2 or 3 tablespoons olive oil in a non-stick frying pan. Fry the tuna steaks for 4 or 5 minutes on each side. Season with salt and pepper. Reserve in a very cool oven – 65°C.

Throw away the cooking oil and deglaze the pan with 3 tablespoons of sherry vinegar. Reserve.

In another pan, brown the garlic slices in tablespoons of olive oil over a low heat. Season with salt.

Pour the reserved vinegar deglazing into the pan with the garlic. Raise the temperature slightly for between 30 to 60 seconds. Then pour over the tuna steaks.

Turbot au Fenouil
Turbot with Fennel

Serves 4
Preparation : 25 minutes
    Cooking : 15 minutes

- 4 turbot filets weighing together about 800g (1¾lb)
- 6 good-sized tomatoes
- 1 bulb fennel
- juice of 4 lemons
- 30cl (10fl oz) fish stock
- 4 finely sliced shallots
- 1 clove garlic – crushed
- 50g (2oz) crème fraîche
- olive oil
- salt, pepper, thyme

Wash the fillets under the tap. Dab dry with absorbent kitchen paper.

Wash the fennel. Cut into fine strips.

Drop the tomatoes in boiling water for 30 seconds, peel and deseed. Cut the flesh into strips.

Brown the fennel, garlic and shallots in a casserole with olive oil. Then cover and sweat a few minutes.

In a medium-sized casserole, heat the lemon juice and fish stock. Season with salt and pepper. Add the thyme. Poach the turbot fillets in the liquid for 7 minutes. Reserve and keep warm.

Reduce the liquid by a quarter, then add the crème fraîche.

Add the tomatoes at the last moment to the garlic and shallots.

Arrange the vegetables on the serving dish. Then lay out the fillets and coat with the sauce.

Turbot à l'Oseille
Turbot with Sorrel

Serves 4
Preparation : 20 minutes
    Cooking : 40 minutes

- 4 turbot fillets
- 100g (4oz) sorrel
- 100g (4oz) crème fraîche
- 25cl (9fl oz) dry white wine
- 25cl (9fl oz) fish stock
- 2 egg yolks
- 2 bay leaves – crumbled
- olive oil
- salt, pepper

Wash the fillets under the tap. Dab dry with absorbent kitchen paper.

Coat an oven dish with olive oil and arrange the fillets on it. Season with salt and pepper. Add the bay leaves. Pour the wine over the top.

Cook for 20 minutes in a fairly hot oven (Mk.5 – 190°C). Reserve and keep warm.

In the meantime, select the best leaves of the sorrel and remove the fibrous stalks. Brown over a very low heat in a pan with a little olive oil.

Reduce the fish stock by half. Then in a bain-marie, beat the stock, crème fraîche and egg yolks with a whisk.

Lay a bed of sorrel on the bottom of the serving dish. Place the fillets on top and coat with the sauce.

SHELLFISH

Queues de Langoustines au Poivre Vert
Langoustines with Green Peppercorns

Recommended side dishes : Leek clafoutis
                          Artichokes provençale

Serves 4
Preparation : 25 minutes
    Cooking : 20 minutes

- 500g (1lb) langoustines
- 3 shallots – sliced
- 20cl (7fl oz) dry white wine
- 50g (2oz) crème fraîche
- olive oil
- 2 tablespoons green peppercorns

In a large pot over a low heat, fry the shallots in a tablespoon of olive oil until translucent.

Add the white wine and simmer for 2 minutes.

Then add the langoustines and cook over a high heat for 5 minutes.

Take out the langoustines and reserve on a serving dish.

Add the peppercorns to the cooking juices and reduce by half.

Turn down the heat and add the crème fraîche. Cook for 2 minutes. Reserve and keep warm.

Peel the langoustines. Add the tails to the sauce and heat for 2 to 3 minutes before serving.

Homards Martiniquais
Lobster Martinique

Recommended side dishes : Skewered vegetables provençale
                          Tomato flan

Serves 4
Preparation : 10 minutes
   Cooking : 25 minutes

- 2 lobsters weighing 500 to 700g (1 to 1½lb)
- 1.5kg (3¼lb) tomatoes
- 12 cloves garlic – crushed
- 4 tablespoons olive oil
- 2 tablespoons freshly chopped parsley
- ½ glass rum
- salt, freshly ground pepper

Blanch the tomatoes in boiling water for 30 seconds. Peel and deseed.

Heat the olive oil in a large casserole. Add the lobsters, cook for 10 minutes turning frequently.

Pour the rum into the casserole and flambé.

Add the garlic. Then, after a couple of minutes, add the tomatoes and the parsley.

Reduce the heat, cover and allow to simmer gently for 15 minutes.

Moules à la Crème de Soja
Mussels with Soya Cream

Serves 4
Preparation : 10 minutes
   Cooking : 20 minutes

- 2kg (4½lb) cleaned mussels
- 6 shallots – finely sliced
- 20cl (7fl oz) dry white wine
- 40cl (14fl oz) soya cream
- olive oil
- sea salt, freshly ground pepper, Herbes de Provence

Clean the mussels in several changes of water. Remove their beards. Immerse in a large pan of fresh water. Throw away those mussels that rise to the surface, are broken or do not close when tapped.

In a large pan, brown the shallots in 3 tablespoons olive oil over a low heat. Season with pepper and stir with a wooden spoon.

Add the white wine, 1 teaspoon sea salt and 1 teaspoon Herbes de Provence. Bring to the boil and leave to cook for 2 minutes.

Pour the mussels into the large pan and cover. Turn the heat to maximum. Leave to cook for approximately 5 minutes. Stir frequently. Shake a few times until the mussels have opened.

Turn the heat well down so the mussels barely simmer. Add the cream of soya and stir. Cover and allow to cook for a further 1 minute.

Serve with a ladle into soup plates.

Huîtres Pochées sur Lit de Poireaux
Poached Oysters on a Bed of Leeks

Serves 4
Preparation : 20 minutes
   Cooking : 25 minutes

- 2 dozen medium oysters
- 3 leek whites
- 3 tablespoons crème fraîche
- 3 shallots – sliced
- 1 glass dry white wine
- olive oil
- salt, freshly ground pepper

In a casserole, brown the shallots with 1 tablespoon of olive oil. Add the white wine. Season with salt and pepper. Reduce by a third and reserve.

Clean the leeks. Cut each leek into 2 or 3 sections and then slice down their length into juliennes. Fry over a low heat in olive oil. Cover and sweat. Reserve and keep warm

Open the oysters (use a steel glove and special knife if possible, to avoid the risk of injury). Detach them from their shells and conserve half the liquid, adding it to the wine mixture.

Place the casserole over a medium heat and poach the oysters for 2 minutes. Remove them with a slotted spoon, reserve and keep warm.

Reduce the the cooking juices to a quarter. Turn down the heat and add the crème fraîche. Season with pepper.

Lay a bed of leeks on each individual plate and arrange the oysters on top, coating with the sauce.

Serve immediately.

Saint-Jacques à l'Echalote et au Soja
Scallops with Shallots and Cream of Soya

Recommended side dishes : Braised leeks
Broccoli
Extra fine French beans

Serves 4
Preparation : 5 minutes
   Cooking : 10 minutes

- 16 scallops
- 8 shallots – sliced
- 15cl (5fl oz) dry white wine
- 4 tablespoons olive oil
- 20cl (7fl oz) cream of soya
- 2 teaspoons Herbes de Provence
- salt, freshly ground pepper, cayenne

Fry the shallots over a gentle heat, stirring occasionally for 5 minutes till they are translucent.

Season with salt, pepper and cayenne. Sprinkle with Herbes de Provence.

Add the scallops. Raise the heat slightly and brown for a minute each side. Slowly add the wine. Stir and leave to simmer for 1 minute.

Add the soya cream. Allow to simmer for a further minute.

Serve immediately.

SIDEDISHES

Having decided on the main dish for the meal, the cook is then left with the problem of deciding which side dish to choose.

For various reasons, there is a natural tendency to produce what is quickly prepared and what is familiar. As a result, the cook tends to produce the same old dishes time and again. This is a pity, because the variety of vegetables available to us throughout the year, is greater than it has ever been.

For this reason, many of the main dishes in this book suggest side dishes to accompany them. A significant number of these dishes feature as recipes in this section (see opposite). They cover a wide selection of vegetables and range from the simple and traditional, to the more elaborate Gratinée Dishes, which can stand on their own as a light meal, eaten perhaps with a salad.

Vegetables are of course delicious when steamed, then dressed with olive oil or a vinaigrette (see p.275). Steamed for about 20 minutes they will not only be tender, they will also be highly nutritious. For someone looking for convenience, a small electric steamer is an excellent investment and not expensive.

Vegetables particularly suited for cooking this way, are listed below:
Asparagus, Aubergines, Broad Beans, Small Broad Beans, Broccoli, Brussel Sprouts, Cabbage, Celeriac, Courgettes, Chicory,Cauliflower, Fennel, French Beans, Leeks, Mangetout, Mushrooms, Peppers, Petits Pois, Salsify, Spinach and Tomatoes.

Artichauts à la Provençale
Artichokes Provençale

Serves 4
Preparation : 15 minutes
 Cooking : 2 hrs

- 8 artichokes
- 3 onions – sliced
- 3 cloves garlic – crushed
- 3 tablespoons olive oil
- 1 sprig of thyme
- 3 bay leaves
- salt, freshly ground pepper

Remove the hard outer leaves of the artichokes and cut the remainder down to the heart. Cook for 30 minutes in boiling salted water. Put the water to one side.

In a casserole, heat the olive oil and fry the onions over a gentle heat. Add the garlic in the last minutes. Season with salt and pepper.

Add the artichokes, thyme and bay leaves. Cover with the hot water put on one side. Allow to boil gently for about 1 hour 30 minutes.

Gratin d'Aubergines à la Tomate
Aubergine Gratin with Tomato

This dish may be served hot, luke-warm or even cold. It can also be served as a starter.

Serves 4/5
Preparation : 20 minutes
    Cooking : 55 minutes

- 1kg (2¼lb) aubergines
- 500g (1lb) tomato coulis (Recipe no.2)
- 500g (1lb) tomatoes, blanched, skinned, deseeded and diced
- 4 cloves garlic – crushed
- 1 tablespoon Herbes de Provence
- 2 tablespoons olive oil
- 2 tablespoons freshly chopped basil
- 4 cloves garlic
- 200g (7oz) grated Gruyère cheese
- 200g (7oz) Mozzarella cheese – sliced
- olive oil
- Herbes de Provence
- 2 tablespoons freshly chopped basil
- salt, freshly ground pepper

Cut the aubergines down their length into slices 1cm (½in) thick. Cook in a steamer for 15 to 20 minutes. Allow to drain for a few moments.

Prepare the tomato coulis (see below).

Brush olive oil onto an ovenware dish. Arrange the sliced aubergine over the bottom.

Spread some of the coulis liberally over the top and sprinkle with grated Gruyère. Arrange another layer of aubergine slices over the top. Coat again with tomato coulis and sprinkle with grated Gruyère cheese. Continue until the supply of aubergine slices is exhausted.

With the final layer of coulis, cover with Mozzarella cheese slices ½cm (¼in) thick and sprinkle with Herbes de Provence.

Place in a pre-heated oven (Mk.2½ – 160°C) for 35 minutes. Serve either hot, luke warm or cold.

To make the coulis:

Pour boiling water over the tomatoes. After 30 seconds, pour off the water and peel the tomatoes. Remove the seeds and dice the flesh. Place in a liquidizer.

Add the crushed garlic, 1 tablespoon Herbes de Provence, 2 tablespoons olive oil and 2 tablespoons of freshly chopped basil. Liquidize into a purée.

Endives Braisées
Braised Chicory

Serves 4
Preparation : 5 minutes
   Cooking : 1 hr 10 minutes

- 8 heads of chicory
- olive oil
- salt, freshly ground pepper

Cook the chicory in boiling salted water for 50 minutes. Drain well.

Cut in half and fry the chicory in olive oil for 10 to 15 minutes.

Season with salt and pepper.

Serve.

Fenouils Braisés
Braised Fennel

Serves 4
Preparation : 5 minutes
      Cooking : 1 hr 15 minutes

- 4 fennel heads
- olive oil
- salt, freshly ground pepper

Cook the fennel for 60 minutes in boiling salted water. Drain well.

Heat 3 tablespoons of olive oil in a pan. Add the fennel and cook over a gentle heat for 15 minutes, turning regularly. Season with salt and pepper.

Poireaux à l'Etouffée
Braised Leeks

Serves 4
Preparation : 10 minutes
    Cooking : 40 minutes

- 1kg (2¼lb) leeks
- olive oil

Remove the roots of the leeks. Remove the green part of stem 2cm (1in) below the point where it changes colour. Throw away the outer leaves and ensure there is no sand embedded in the plant. Wash and drain.

Chop the leeks into 3cm (1in) lengths.

Heat gently 3 tablespoons of olive oil in a large pan. Then add the leeks. Stir well, cover and simmer for about 35 minutes. Occasionally remove the lid to stir. Season with salt and pepper.

Check to see whether the leeks are properly cooked.

When very tender, remove from the heat and serve on a warm plate.

Purée de Brocolis au Soja
Broccoli Purée with Soya Cream

Serves 4
Preparation : 5 minutes
   Cooking : 25 minutes

- 800g (1¾lb) broccoli
- 20cl (7fl oz) soya cream
- salt, freshly ground pepper

Cook the broccoli for 25 minutes in a steamer.

Transfer to a bowl. Season with salt and pepper, then add the soya cream and stir together thoroughly.

Crush with a fork or purée in a food processor.

Serve in a warm dish.

Choux de Bruxelles à la Gersoise
Brussel Sprouts from Gers

Serves 4
Preparation : 10 minutes
   Cooking : 20 minutes

- 1kg (2¼lb) Brussels sprouts
- 2 cubes beef stock
- goose fat
- freshly ground pepper, nutmeg

Clean and wash the sprouts.

Bring 3 to 4 litres (6 to 8 pints) of water to the boil. Dissolve 2 stock cubes in the boiling water and season with pepper.

Add the sprouts. When the water has come back to the boil, lower the heat. Allow to boil gently for about 12 minutes.

Drain the sprouts.

In a frying pan or wok, melt 2 tablespoons goose fat over a medium heat. Add the sprouts and sauté until lightly browned.

Transfer to a warm shallow dish and grate a little nutmeg on the top and serve.

Gratinée de Chou-fleur
Cauliflower Gratin

This dish may also be served as a starter or main dish.

Serves 5
Preparation : 15 minutes
    Cooking : 30 minutes

- 1 large cauliflower – between 1.2 to 1.5kg (2½ – 3lb)
- 250g (9oz) grated Gruyère cheese
- 40cl (14fl oz) double cream
- salt, freshly ground pepper

Wash the cauliflower. Cut the fleurets from the stem and cook for 15 minutes in a large pan of salted, boiling water. Drain well.

In a bowl, mix the grated Gruyère and the double cream. Season generously with pepper.

Oil a shallow oven dish. Arrange the fleurets and pour the cream mixture over the top.

Place under a well- heated grill for 10 to 12 minutes.

Serve very hot in the shallow oven dish.

Purée de Céleri
Celeriac Purée

Serves 4
Preparation : 10 minutes
    Cooking : 1 hr 15 minutes

- 1 celeriac
- 1 lemon
- 30cl (10fl oz) double cream
- salt, freshly ground pepper, nutmeg

Peel and wash the celeriac.

Cut into large cubes. Cook for a good hour in boiling salted water together with the lemon cut into quarters.

Drain the celeriac and discard the pieces of lemon.

Add the cream to the celeriac. Season with salt and pepper. Sprinkle with the grated nutmeg.

Simmer over a very gentle heat, until the cream has been absorbed by the celeriac. Transfer to the blender and make into a purée.

Adjust the seasoning and serve on a warm dish.

Tapenade
Crushed Olives with Capers and Anchovies

This dish should be stored in a large sealed jar and kept
in the refrigerator. It can be used with many other dishes
or just simply as a spread on toast made from 'pain intégrale'
– bread made with unrefined flour.
This recipe makes 800g (28oz) of Tapenade.

Phase 2

Preparation : 10 minutes
No cooking

- 250g (9oz) stoned black olives
- 100g (4oz) anchovy fillets
- 100g (4oz) tuna in olive oil
- 200g (8oz) capers
- 1 tablespoon Dijon Mustard
- 1 glass brandy – 5cl (2fl oz)
- 20cl (7fl oz) olive oil
- salt, freshly ground pepper, paprika

Put all the ingredients into a blender and reduce to a paste.

Jambon aux Courgettes et au Parmesan
Cured Ham with Courgettes and Parmesan

To make this into a main dish, just add a couple of large free-range eggs fried in goose fat.

Serves 4
Preparation : 15 minutes
    Cooking : 20 minutes

- 8 slices of cured ham
- 4 nice courgettes
- 4 large tomatoes
- 100g (4oz) grated Parmesan cheese
- olive oil
- chopped parsley
- salt, freshly ground pepper

Dice the courgettes.

Pour boiling water over the tomatoes for 30 seconds. Drain, peel and deseed. Dice the tomato flesh.

Fry the courgettes and the tomatoes over a medium heat for about 12 minutes, stirring frequently. Season with salt and pepper.

Gradually add the grated Parmesan to the pan, together with another tablespoon of olive oil. Leave to cook over a low heat for 5 to 6 minutes, stirring occasionally.

Arrange the slices of ham in individual plates. Serve the courgettes with the cheese mixture on top. Sprinkle with chopped parsley.

Quiche Rustique
Farmhouse Quiche

This dish may also be served as a main dish with salad, or as a starter.

Serves 4/5
Preparation : 15 minutes
    Cooking : 1 hr 10 minutes

- 5 eggs
- 600g (1¼lb) leeks
- 150g (5oz) diced streaky bacon
- 1 large onion – sliced
- 300g (10oz) half-fat crème fraîche
- 200g (7oz) grated Gouda cheese
- olive oil
- salt, freshly ground pepper, nutmeg

Wash the leeks and discard the thick green parts. Cut into slices 1 to 2cm (½in) thick.

Fry the diced streaky bacon in a large frying pan over a gentle heat, to extract as much fat as possible. Reserve and keep warm.

In a casserole, heat 2 tablespoons of olive oil. Add the onion and leeks and cook over a low heat. Stir well. Leave to cook slowly for 20 minutes, stirring from time to time. Season with salt and pepper.

Break the eggs into a bowl. Beat together with the crème fraîche. Add a little salt, pepper and freshly grated nutmeg. Add the grated cheese and mix well.

Using the slotted spoon, remove the diced streaky bacon, onions and leeks from their respective pans and transfer to the bowl containing the egg and crème fraîche mixture. Mix well.

Pour the preparation into 28cm (11in) flan dish that has been brushed with olive oil. Cook au bain-marie in a warm oven (Mk.2½ – 160°C) for 40 minutes.

Serve luke warm.

Tomates Fraîches Farcies au Salpicon
Fresh Tomatoes with Spicy Filling

Serves 4
Preparation : 20 minutes
No cooking

- 5/6 tomatoes
- 200g (7oz) tuna in brine
- 50g (2oz) anchovy fillets
- 50g (2oz) capers
- 50g (2oz) gherkins
- 1 egg yolk
- 1 teaspoon mustard
- olive oil
- 2 cloves garlic
- salt, freshly ground pepper, paprika

Grate the cloves of garlic.

Dice the gherkins very finely.

Make a small amount of mayonnaise with the egg yolk, the teaspoon of mustard and the olive oil.

Blend the tuna, anchovy fillets and capers in a food processor. Mix with the mayonnaise, grated garlic and chopped gherkin, into a creamy mixture. Add a little olive oil if necessary.

Adjust the seasoning with salt, pepper and paprika. The salpicon stuffing is now ready.

Cut off the tops of the tomatoes, hollow them out with a small spoon and stuff with the salpicon.

Arrange on a dish or on individual plates and leave in a cool place for 2 to 3 hours before serving.

Clafoutis de Poireaux
Leek Clafoutis

This dish may also be served as a starter or as a main dish in a light meal.

Serves 4
Preparation : 15 minutes
    Cooking : 1 hr 10 minutes

- 5 nice leeks
- 300g (10oz) fromage frais
- 3 whole eggs + 1 yolk
- 1 clove garlic – crushed with a little ginger
- 100g (4oz) Gruyère cheese
- salt, freshly ground pepper

Prepare the leeks. Cut the white part of the leek into sections 3 to 4cm (1in) long. Cook in a steamer for 20 minutes. Drain well.

In a bowl, beat the eggs with the yolk and then add the fromage frais, stirring in well. Then stir in the Gruyère cheese and the crushed garlic and ginger.

Arrange the leeks in the bottom of an oiled 28cm (11in) ovenware dish. Pour the egg mixture over the top.

Put in a very cool oven and bake for 45 minutes (Mk.¼ – 100°C).

Sprinkle the rest of the gruyè re cheese over the top of the dish and place under the grill for a few minutes, until the cheese turns crunchy.

Gratinée d'Oignons
Onion Gratinée

Serves 5
Preparation : 15 minutes
    Cooking : 55 minutes

- 600g (1¼lb) onions – sliced
- 150g (5oz) crème fraîche
- 6 eggs
- 100g (4oz) grated Gruyère cheese
- 100g (4oz) Mozzarella cheese – thinly sliced
- olive oil
- salt, freshly ground pepper

Fry the onions in a large frying pan in 3 tablespoons olive oil over a gentle heat, stirring continuously. Cook until most of their moisture has evaporated and the onions are golden brown. Season with salt and pepper.

In a large bowl, beat together the eggs, grated cheese and crème fraîche. Season sparingly with salt and pepper. Using a slotted spoon, transfer the onions from pan to bowl. Stir until completely mixed.

Pour the mixture into a shallow oven dish and cook for 40 minutes in the oven (Mk.½ – 130°C).

Slice the Mozzarella as finely as possible, and cover the dish with the slices.

Place the dish under the grill until the cheese melts.

Champignons Persillés
Parsley Mushrooms

This dish may also be used as a starter.

Serves 4
Preparation : 20 minutes
    Cooking : 15 minutes

- 800g (1¾lb) fairly large button mushrooms
- 6 cloves garlic – sliced
- 2 tablespoons freshly chopped parsley
- olive oil
- salt, freshly ground pepper

Remove the base of the stalks. Wash and wipe clean. Drain well. Slice lengthways.

Heat 3 tablespoons olive oil in a frying pan over a gentle heat. Fry the mushrooms and stir well with a wooden spoon.

When the mushrooms have lost their water, throw away the cooking juices and add a further 3 tablespoons of olive oil. Season with salt and pepper. Stir for about 1 minute over a low heat.

Scrape the mushrooms to the side, then tilt the pan so that all the cooking oil drains to the empty part. In the oily part of the pan, brown the crushed garlic and the chopped parsley, then mix well with the mushrooms.

Serve immediately.

Ratatouille
Ratatouille

This dish is even better when reheated after being allowed to stand.

Serves 5/6
Preparation : 20 minutes
    Cooking : 60 minutes

- 3 good-sized aubergines
- 3 red peppers
- 1kg (2¼lb) tomatoes – skinned
- 3 courgettes
- 3 onions
- 4 cloves garlic
- Herbes de Provence
- olive oil
- salt, freshly ground pepper, cayenne

Halve the red peppers down their length. Remove the stalk and the seeds. Place under the grill skin side up until slightly charred. Allow to cool and remove the skin. Cut into strips.

Cut the aubergines into thick 2cm (1in) cubes.

Over a gentle heat, fry in a casserole or a wok with some olive oil for 30 minutes. Stir regularly.

Cut the courgettes into large dice and fry in olive oil. Stir regularly.

Cut the tomatoes into pieces and cook in an open casserole with some olive oil, until they have lost their liquid.

Fry the onions and the garlic over a very gentle heat in some olive oil.

Put all the vegetables without their cooking juices in a large pan.

Pour about 15cl (5fl oz) olive oil over the top. Sprinkle with Herbes de Provence.

Season with salt, pepper and a pinch of cayenne pepper.

Stir well and simmer with no cover for 15 minutes over a very low heat.

Serve either hot or cold.

Brochettes Provençales
Skewered Vegetables Provençale

Serves 4
Preparation : 20 minutes
     Cooking : 15 – 20 minutes

- 8 small firm tomatoes
- 4 large button mushrooms
- 2 large onions
- 2 red peppers
- olive oil
- salt, freshly ground pepper, Herbes de Provence

Cut the tomatoes in half and the onions and mushrooms in quarters.

Cut the peppers in half. Remove the stem and the seeds, then cut into 3cm (1in) squares.

To make up a skewer, thread ½ tomato, ¼ onion, a square of pepper, ¼ mushroom, ½ tomato, and so on – completing the row with ½ tomato.

Brush with olive oil. Season with salt and pepper. Sprinkle with Herbes de Provence.

Arrange the skewers on an oven pan and place the pan about 10cm (4 in) below the grill.

Grill, turning the skewer regularly a turn at a time.

Epinards à la Crème de Soja
Spinach with Soya Cream

Serves 4
Preparation : 15 minutes
    Cooking : 45 minutes

- 2kg (4½lb) spinach
- 2 tablespoons goose fat
- 1 bunch of parsley
- 20cl (7fl oz) soya cream
- salt, freshly ground pepper

Wash the spinach and remove the stalks. Drain.

In a casserole, melt 2 tablespoons of goose fat. Then add the spinach.

Cover and allow to cook for 12 minutes over a very gentle heat. Season with salt and add the bunch of parsley. Stir.

Cover again and leave to cook for 30 minutes.

Transfer the spinach to a food processor and add the soya cream. Blend.

Return to the pan and warm the vegetable mixture gently, for no more than a minute to prevent the soya cream coagulating.

Season with salt and pepper.

Tagliatelles au Pistou
Tagliatelle with Pesto

This dish make a good starter or main dish for a light meal.

Phase 2

Serves 4/5
Preparation : 15 minutes
    Cooking : 10 minutes

- 500g (1lb) tagliatelle made from unrefined flour (farine intégrale)
- 4 cloves garlic – crushed
- 250g (9oz) grated Parmesan cheese
- 15 leaves basil
- 7 tablespoons olive oil
- 75g (3oz) pine nuts
- salt, freshly ground pepper

Boil salted water in a tall large pan. Add 1 teaspoon of olive oil.

Crush the garlic and chopped basil leaves together in a mortar, until a paste is formed. Add olive oil little by little and mix together with a wooden spoon. Then add the grated Parmesan cheese. (Alternatively, put all the ingredients in a food processor and blend). Season very lightly with salt and pepper.

When the water is bubbling fiercely, add the tagliatelli. Cook until 'al dente' – between 6 to 12 minutes, depending on the make.

When the tagliatelli are cooked, turn off the heat and add a cupful of cold water to the pan to arrest further cooking. Drain in a colander and serve in individual plates.

Top with the sauce and add the pine nuts.

Flan à la tomate
Tomato Flan

This dish can also be served as a starter or as a main dish.

Serves 4/5
Preparation : 15 minutes
   Cooking : 55 minutes

- 8 to 10 tomatoes (depending on size)
- 5 eggs + 1 yolk
- 20cl (7fl oz) double cream
- 150g (5oz) grated Gruyère cheese
- 100g (4oz) Mozzarella – finely sliced
- 1 tablespoon of freshly chopped basil

Cover the tomatoes with boiling water for 30 seconds. Peel and remove the seeds.

Dice the flesh and drain for a good 30 minutes, to ensure they lose as much water as possible.

Melt the grated Gruyère in the double cream over a gentle heat and stir continuously with a wooden spoon.

Arrange the diced tomatoes evenly in an oiled 28cm (11in) ovenware flan dish.

Beat the eggs and yolk, the creamed Gruyère and the basil. Season generously with salt and pepper. Pour over the diced tomatoes in the earthenware dish.

Bake in a very cool oven (Mk.½ – 130°C) for 40 minutes.

Before serving, spread the slices of Mozzarella on top of the dish. Place under the grill for a few minutes.

Chou à l'Ancienne
Traditional Cabbage

The liquid produced during the cooking may be retained to make a soup, by liquidizing with the remainder of the cabbage.

Serves 5/6
Preparation : 15 minutes
    Cooking : 2 hrs 20 minutes

- 1 large cabbage – about 1.5kg (3¼lb)
- 250g (9oz) diced streaky bacon
- 2 onions – sliced
- bouquet garni (bay, thyme and parsley)
- 2 beef stock cubes
- goose fat
- salt, freshly ground pepper

Heat a large pan full of salted water. Remove the outer leaves of the cabbage. Quarter. Remove the stem and the larger stalks.

Blanch for 20 minutes. Drain well.

In a large casserole, melt 1 tablespoon goose fat and gently fry the diced streaky bacon over a low heat. Then add the sliced onions and fry until golden brown.

Add the cabbage leaves, bouquet garni and crumble the stock cubes over the top. Cover with water. Season lightly with pepper and salt.

Cover and boil gently for 2 hours.

Turn out onto a shallow dish, remove the bouquet garni, then serve.

SALADS

To make a good salad, it is essential all the ingredients should be as fresh as possible and of the best quality.

The seasoning should include salt. In France, I recommend Sel de Guérande: in England, Maldon Sea Salt is very good.

Vinegar is also an essential ingredient: it should be made from red wine. And it need not be expensive, for it is quite easily made at home. Stoneware pots with a wooden tap made specifically for the purpose are easily obtainable. All you need to do is soak the wooden tap well before inserting it in the pot with its bung, pour in a bottle of wine and add the culture. From then on, just add all your wine remains – white or red – and keep the pot in the cool.

Sherry vinegar is often used for deglazing the cooking pan, but its distinctive flavour gives added character to a salad.

Balsamic vinegar, with its very particular character, is generally used cut with ordinary wine vinegar to make its effect more subtle.

Another very important ingredient in a dressing, is mustard. There are many different types, but the one most used in France is Moutarde Forte de Dijon.

Then of course, we have the vegetable oils. Three main types are used normally:

Sunflower oil, which has to be purified to make its very strong flavour more acceptable.

Olive oil, which should state on its label that it is Virgin and that it is from the First Cold Pressing. When it fulfils these two conditions, olive oil is the queen of oils and should be used in abundance, because it is very good for you.

Walnut Oil, which is very aromatic, makes a remarkable difference to a salad. The only drawback to its use is that it does not keep very long, once the bottle is opened. So to prevent it becoming rancid relatively quickly, it must be kept in the fridge. For this reason, it is advisable to purchase it only in small amounts – 25 to 50cl (9 to 18fl oz).

Mixed herbs are not essential but they are always welcome. The classic herbs are parsley, tarragon, basil and chives.

When we think of Spices, the first one that comes to mind is pepper, either freshly ground or crushed in a pestle to conserve its wonderful aroma. However, there are others that make a valuable contribution to a vinaigrette. A discreet pinch of curry powder gives an added sense of character, and you can afford to be rather more generous with mild paprika.

And then last – but by no means least – we have garlic and Herbes de Provence. To those that come from the South East of France, they are indispensable elements in any salad and as far as garlic is concerned, extremely good for you. However, those that find it too pungent can always use it more sparingly – just enough to give their vinaigrette that little air of mystery.

Farandole de Salades
Improvised Salads

Here are a few ideas for salads that are normally improvised according to the ingredients that happen to be available at the time.

Phase 1:

Artichoke and asparagus salad

Avocado salad, tomatoes, tuna, hard-boiled eggs, gruyère cheese, lettuce

Cucumber and tomato salad

Curly endive salad with diced bacon

Endive salad with roquefort cheese or walnuts

French bean and smoked salmon salad

Fresh spinach salad, with walnuts and gruyère cheese

Green salad
(lettuce, lamb's lettuce, watercress, dandelion, lollo rosso, lollo biondo, oakleaf lettuce, cos, frisée . . .), plain or mixed, with or without herbs, but always with a good vinaigrette.

Green salad, extra-thin French beans, tomatoes

Green salad with warm goat's cheese

Palm heart salad

Tomatoes, basil, goat's cheese (or feta)

Phase 2:

Lentil salad with shallots
(the shallots should be sliced very thinly and the vinaigrette should have a generous dose of mustard)

Chickpea salad with a pinch of cumin

Red kidney bean salad with a pinch of ground coriander and a generous sprinkling of olive oil

Salade d'Asperges au Saumon Fumé
Asparagus Salad with Smoked Salmon

Serves 4
Preparation : 20 minutes
    Cooking : 50 minutes

- 800g (1¾lb) asparagus
- 200g smoked salmon – thinly sliced
- 4 sprigs dill – chopped
- 4 slices lemon
- 20cl (7fl oz) whipping cream
- 1½ tablespoons strong Dijon mustard

Wash and peel the asparagus. Cook in salted water for about 20 minutes or until tender (test with the point of a knife). Drain and reserve.

Whip the cream until stiff. Stir in the mustard and chopped dill.

Roll the salmon slices around the asparagus near their tips.

Arrange the asparagus attractively on a rectangular dish.

Coat them with the sauce and decorate with the dill and lemon slices.

Salade d'Avocat aux Poivrons
Avocado Salad with Peppers

Serves 4
Preparation : 15 minutes
    Cooking : 15 to 20 minutes

- 2 ripe avocados
- 2 red peppers
- 4 chicory heads
- a few leaves assorted lettuce
- 2 tablespoons chopped parsley
- 20 black olives – stoned
- vinaigrette provençale (see p.275)
- lemon

Put the red peppers in a pre-heated oven (Mk.6 – 200°C) and bake for 20 minutes until the skin blisters. Cool and peel the skin. Cut the flesh into thin strips.

Halve the avocados lengthways, stone, peel and slice. Sprinkle with lemon juice to prevent them going brown. Stone the olives and chop.

Prepare the assorted lettuce leaves.

Cut the chicory into slices ½cm (¼in) thick.

To serve, arrange the lettuce, avocado, chicory and red peppers on individual plates. Pour the vinaigrette on the top and sprinkle with parsley and chopped olives

Salade de Fèves au Bacon
Bacon and Broad Bean Salad

Serves 4   Phase 2
Preparation : 20 minutes
    Cooking : 25 minutes

- 1.5kg (3¼lb) fresh broad beans
- 150g (5oz) bacon
- 1 onion
- 1 bunch fresh mint
- 15cl (5fl oz) olive oil
- 1 tablespoon balsamic vinegar
- salt, freshly ground pepper

Shell the beans and cook for 15 to 20 minutes in a large pan of salted water. Drain, allow to cool and remove the fine membrane that covers the bean by pinching it between thumb and index finger.

Peel, halve and slice the onion.

Chop about ten leaves of mint very finely.

Cut the slices of bacon into 4 and brown in a non-stick pan with a little olive oil and the sliced onion.

Make the vinaigrette in a bowl: add salt and pepper to the balsamic vinegar, then add the olive oil and mix vigorously.

Add the beans, bacon, onion and mint. Toss and serve on individual plates. Decorate with the rest of the mint leaves and serve.

Salade de Brocolis aux Amandes
Broccoli Salad with Almonds

Serves 4
Preparation : 15 minutes
    Cooking : 15 minutes

- 500g (1lb) broccoli
- 75g (3oz) almonds
- 2 red peppers
- 2 tablespoons chopped parsley
- vinaigrette provençale (see p.275)

Put the red peppers into a pre-heated oven (Mk.6 – 200°C) or steamer until blistered. Cool and peel. Cut into thin strips.

Divide the broccoli into fleurets and cook in a steamer for 15 minutes. Allow to cool.

On individual plates, arrange the broccoli with almonds and strips of red pepper on the top.

Pour the vinaigrette over the dish and sprinkle with chopped parsley.

Remoulade de Céleri à l'Avocat
Celeriac and Avocado Remoulade

Serves 4
Preparation : 20 minutes
No cooking

- 1 large celeriac weighing about 600g (1¼lb)
- 1 ripe avocado
- 200g (8oz) yoghurt
- 1 dozen black olives – stoned
- 1 lemon
- 1 tablespoon strong mustard
- 3 tablespoons olive oil
- 2 cloves garlic
- 1 tablespoon powdered wheat germ
- 1 tablespoon chopped parsley
- salt, freshly ground pepper, ground coriander

Peel the celeriac, cut into manageable lumps and grate. Sprinkle lemon juice over the top to prevent it oxidizing and going brown.

Crush the garlic. Stone the avocado and scoop out the flesh.

To make the sauce:
Put the avocado, yoghurt, mustard, wheat germ, olive oil, garlic and black olives into a food processor. Season with salt, pepper. add a few pinches of coriander and blend for a few seconds to obtain a sauce with the consistency of a mayonnaise.

Mix the celeriac with the sauce.

Arrange in a serving dish or on individual plates, and decorate with chopped parsley.

Poulet en Salade
Chicken Salad

This dish may be served either with vinaigrette or with mayonnaise.

Serves 4
Preparation : 20 minutes
    Cooking : 20 minutes

- 1 small lettuce
- 4 sticks celery
- 4 boneless chicken breasts
- 4 hard-boiled eggs
- 24 black olives – stoned
- 24 green olives – stoned
- sweet paprika
- salt, freshly ground pepper, vinaigrette and/or mayonnaise
- goose fat

Cook the chicken in goose fat for no more than 20 minutes over a very low heat. Season with salt, pepper. Allow to cool and cut into slices 2cm (1in) thick.

Take the best leaves of the lettuce and cut into strips.

Chop the celery stalks into small pieces.

Cut the hard-boiled eggs into slices and sprinkle with paprika.

Dress the individual plates with lettuce, chicken, celery, eggs and olives.

Serve with vinaigrette or mayonnaise.

Salade de Pissenlits au Lard et au Fromage
Dandelion Salad with Bacon and Cheese

Serves 4
Preparation : 20 minutes
    Cooking : 5 minutes

- 300g (¾lb) dandelion leaves (or rocket if preferred)
- 200g (8oz) Beaufort cheese
- 150g (5oz) diced smoked bacon
- 2 hard-boiled eggs
- 1clove garlic – crushed
- 12 green olives – stoned
- olive oil vinaigrette
- salt, freshly ground pepper, walnut oil

Clean and wash the dandelion leaves in 3 changes of water. Drain well.

Dice the smoked bacon and blanch for 4 minutes in unsalted boiling water. Drain and dab dry with absorbent kitchen paper. Fry over a gentle heat in a non-stick frying pan until crisp.

Prepare the vinaigrette: dissolve the salt in the vinegar. Add the crushed garlic, pepper and olive oil. Mix well.

Cut the beaufort cheese into cubes and slice the hard-boiled eggs.

Place the dandelion leaves in a large bowl and add the warm diced bacon, cheese and eggs. Toss in the vinaigrette. Add the olives and lace with walnut oil before serving.

Vinaigrette Familiale
French Vinaigrette

Prepared in a bottle or cruet.

- 1 tablespoon strong mustard
- 15cl (5fl oz) wine vinegar
- 20cl (7fl oz) sunflower oil
- 20cl (7fl oz) olive oil
- 1 teaspoon sea salt
- 3 grindings of pepper
- 1clove garlic – crushed
- 1 teaspoon Herbes de Provence
- 3 pinches mild paprika
- 1 small pinch cayenne
- 1 pinch curry powder

Dissolve all the solid ingredients in the vinegar. Add the oils and shake well.

Vinaigrette Provençale: Is very similar to this general recipe. However, it contains only olive oil – 40cl (14fl oz).

Salade Gourmande
Gourmand Salad

Serves 4
Preparation : 25 minutes
    Cooking : 55 minutes

- 400g (1lb) very fine french beans
- 8 scallops
- 200g (7oz) foie gras
- 1 bunch parsley
- balsamic vinaigrette with olive oil
- sea salt, freshly ground pepper

If you cannot use fresh foie gras, then used the tinned version. Cut into 8 thin slices and arrange on a plate. Cover with plastic film and place in the fridge for at least an hour.

Cook the french beans so they remain 'al dente' or slightly firm.

Prepare the vinaigrette: dissolve the salt in the balsamic vinegar and add the pepper and olive oil. Mix well.

Poach the scallops for 5 minutes in water with sea salt and pepper. Drain and reserve.

Just before serving, using a very sharp knife slice the scallops very thinly.

Arrange the french beans edged with the sliced scallops in each plate, and then add the 2 slices of foie gras.

Decorate with parsley and lace with the vinaigrette.

Salade de Champignons
Mushroom Salad

Serves 4/5
Preparation : 20 minutes
    Cooking : 5 minutes

- 500g (1lb) button mushrooms
- 1 egg yolk
- 1 glass olive oil
- 2 lemons
- salt, pepper, mustard
- 1 bunch parsley

Clean the mushrooms well.

In a large pan, add salt and the juice of 1 lemon to 1 litre of water and bring to the boil. Add the mushrooms and leave to cook for 3 or 4 minutes. Drain well and allow to cool.

To make the mayonnaise, whisk together an egg yolk, 1 teaspoon of mustard and then gradually add the olive oil, beating all the time. Season with salt and pepper and then gradually beat in the juice of the second lemon. Reserve in the fridge.

Slice the mushrooms lengthways. Add to mayonnaise and mix well. Sprinkle with chopped parsley and serve.

Salade de Haricots
Red Bean Salad

(V)

Serves 4
Preparation : 20 minutes
   Cooking : 1 hr 30 minutes

- 200g (8oz) red beans
- 200g (8oz) button mushrooms
- 100g (4oz) bean sprouts
- 2 red peppers
- 3 tablespoons chopped basil
- 3 tablespoons chopped parsley
- vinaigrette provençale
- walnut oil

Soak the beans for 12 hours in plenty of water. Cook for 1 hour and 15 minutes in slightly salted water.

Clean the button mushrooms. Slice lengthways and sprinkle with lemon juice to prevent them from turning black.

Put the peppers in a preheated oven (Mk.6 – 200°C) or steamer for 20 minutes until they blister. Cool, peel and cut into narrow slices.

Put the beans, mushrooms, beans sprouts, red pepper, basil and parsley into a bowl or into individual plates.

Add a little walnut oil to the vinaigrette, pour over the top and serve.

Salade de Chou Rouge aux Noix
Red Cabbage Salad with Walnuts

Serves 5
Preparation : 15 minutes
No cooking

- 1 small red cabbage
- 1 onion – thinly sliced
- 2 tablespoons olive oil
- 2 tablespoons red wine vinegar
- 2 teaspoons walnut oil
- 1 teaspoon mustard
- 50g (2oz) walnuts very coarsely chopped
- salt, freshly ground pepper

Remove the coarse outer leaves of the cabbage. Quarter and slice thinly.

Peel the onion and cut into thin slices. Ensure the slices break up into rings.

Prepare the vinaigrette: dissolve the salt and mustard in the vinegar. Add the pepper, olive oil and walnut oil. Mix well.

Put the cabbage in a bowl, add the vinaigrette and walnuts. Toss and serve.

Salade de Cresson aux Lardons
Watercress and Bacon Salad

Serves 4
Preparation : 15 minutes
  Cooking : 12 minutes

- 350g (12oz) watercress
- 100g (4oz) diced streaky bacon
- ½ glass sherry vinegar
- olive oil

Dice the streaky bacon. Blanch for 4 minutes in boiling unsalted water. Drain.

Fry the diced streaky bacon in a non-stick pan over a low heat until the fat has melted.

Sort and wash the watercress. Drain and transfer to a large bowl.

Throw away the melted bacon fat and deglaze the pan with the sherry vinegar. Turn the diced bacon and deglazing over the watercress. Dribble olive oil over the top.

Toss the salad and serve.

DESSERTS

Brouillade de Pommes à la Cannelle
Apple Scramble with Cinnamon

Serves 4
Preparation : 30 minutes
Cooking : 35 minutes

Phase 2

- 8 nice apples
- 3 complete eggs + 3 yolks
- 4 tablespoons fructose
- 5cl (2fl oz) calvados
- 15cl (6fl oz) low-fat crème fraîche
- cinnamon powder

Peel the apples. Quarter and remove the core. Cook in the steamer for about 20 minutes. Drain well.

In a large bowl, beat the egg, yolks and fructose. Add the apples, calvados and crème fraîche. Sprinkle with cinnamon. Continue to beat with a whisk until the mixture has a uniform consistency.

Pour into a large non-stick pan and cook over a very, very low heat – as for making scrambled eggs – stirring continuously with a spatula. Take the pan off the heat and pour the mixture which should still be slightly moist, into low ovenware dishes or ramekins.

Sprinkle over the top with cinnamon and when quite cool, place in the fridge for 2 or 3 hours.

Serve ungarnished or with a chocolate coulis and/or whipped cream.

Soufflé de Pommes Falmbé au Calvados
Apple Soufflé Flambé with Calvados

After this dish has been flamed with calvados, it can be allowed to cool before browning lightly under a hot grill.

Phase 2

Serves 5
Preparation : 30 minutes
    Cooking : 55 minutes

- 12 apples
- 5 egg yolks
- 5 tablespoons fructose
- 20cl (7fl oz) whipping cream
- 1 teaspoon vanilla extract
- 5cl (2fl oz) calvados

Peel the apples. Cut into quarters and remove the core.

Brush an ovenware dish lightly with oil and distribute the apple quarters evenly. Sprinkle 2 tablespoons of fructose over the top.

Bake in a very hot oven (Mk.8 – 230°C) for 25 minutes. Reserve.

In a large bowl, beat the egg yolks with 2 tablespoons of fructose until the mixture begins to turn creamy white.

Whisk the cream until very stiff and add 1 tablespoon of fructose.

Pour away the juice that has drained out of the apples. Then mix together well the apples, beaten eggs, whipped cream and vanilla extract.

Turn into an oiled ovenware dish and cook in a cool oven (Mk.½ – 120°C) for 35 to 40 minutes. Remove from the oven. Flame with calvados and serve.

Bavarois à l'Abricot et son Coulis
Apricot Bavarois with its Coulis

Serves 4
Preparation : 20 minutes
   Cooking : 15 minutes

- 750g (1¾lb) apricots
- 5 leaves of gelatine – or the equivalent of agar-agar
- 25cl (9fl oz) full milk
- 100g (3½oz) fructose
- 20cl (7fl oz) whipping cream
- 5cl (2fl oz) cognac

Cut the apricots in half and remove the stones. Place in a steamer and cook for 10 minutes. Reserve and allow to cool.

Bring the milk to the boil and then allow to cool for 10 minutes.

Immerse the leaves of gelatine in cold water. Squeeze dry and then add to the milk. Stir well and allow to stand for 15 minutes.

Mix 50g (2oz) of fructose with the cream and beat until stiff.

Fold the whipped cream into the milk (which is just beginning to set) and add the cognac. Stir gently with the whisk to obtain a smooth mixture.

Take half the apricots, dice and fold into the mixture.

Pour into ramekins or into rings 8cm (3in) in diameter, and place in the fridge for 6 hours and allow to set.

To make the coulis, combine the remaining apricots and fructose in a food processor. Reserve and keep cool.

Unmould onto individual plates and surround with the coulis.

Soupe d'Abricots
Apricots and Custard

Serves 4
Preparation : 15 minutes
   Cooking : 20 minutes

- 20 nice apricots
- 2 tablespoons fructose
- ½ glass rum

FOR THE CUSTARD:
- 8 egg yolks
- 1 litre (1¾ pints) milk
- 3 tablespoons fructose
- 1 vanilla pod
- sugar-free cocoa powder

Split open the apricots and remove the stones.

Place in a steamer skin-side facing downwards. Sprinkle with 2 tablespoons of fructose and cook for 10 minutes. Allow to drain. Flambé with the rum and allow to cool. Reserve in the fridge.

Bring the milk with the split vanilla pod slowly to the boil. Remove from the heat and allow to cool for 10 minutes.

Beat the egg yolks, adding the warm milk slowly to the mixture. Then whisk briskly.

Return the mixture to a low heat to thicken (preferably au bain-marie), beating constantly. When the custard has the right consistency, allow to cool for a few minutes and add fructose.

Leave in the fridge for several hours.

To serve, place 8 to 10 apricot halves in a shallow dish. Ladle custard over the top and dust with the cocoa powder.

Blanc-manger au Coulis de Framboises
Blanc-mange with Raspberry Coulis

Serves 5   Phase 2
Preparation : 20 minutes
  Cooking : 5 minutes

- 250g (8oz) raspberries
- 400g (14oz) fromage frais – strained
- 30cl (10oz) whipping cream
- 4 tablespoons of sugar-free raspberry jam
- 6 leaves of gelatine (or the equivalent of agar-agar)
- 1 tablespoon fructose
- 1 tablespoon rum

Whip the cream until stiff.

Soften the gelatine leaves in cold water. Squeeze dry and dissolve in the rum which should be slightly warm.

Mix well together the whipped cream, strained fromage frais, rum gelatine and raspberry jam.

Brush the moulds with egg white. Arrange some raspberries at the bottom of each mould and pour the rum mixture over the top and place in the fridge to set.

Prepare the coulis by liquidizing the remaining raspberries with the fructose. Strain through a sieve.

To serve, unmold the bavarois onto individual plates and coat with the coulis.

Mousse au Café
Brazilian Mousse

Serves 6   Phase 2
Preparation : 20 minutes
    Cooking : 10 minutes

- 4 tablespoons instant coffee
- 20cl (7fl oz) whipping cream
- 6 eggs
- 3 leaves gelatine (or the equivalent of agar-agar)
- ½ glass rum
- 100g (3½oz) fructose

In a bain-marie, dissolve the instant coffee in the rum and cream. Add the fructose and dissolve.

Immerse the gelatine in cold water for a few minutes. Remove and squeeze out. Add to the coffee mixture and dissolve. Allow to cool.

Break the eggs and separate the whites from the yolks.

Add a pinch of salt to the whites and whisk until very stiff.

Mix the coffee cream with the egg yolks. Fold the whites carefully into the coffee mixture with a metal spoon.

Put in a fridge for 5 to 6 hours.

Before serving, sprinkle with freshly ground coffee beans.

Crème Catalane aux Framboises Fraîches
Catalan Cream with Fresh Raspberries

Serves 4

Preparation : 15 minutes

Cooking : 60 minutes

Phase 2

- 1 punnet of raspberries
- 5 egg yolks
- 350g (12oz) crème fraîche
- 15cl (5fl oz) full cream milk
- 80g fructose
- 1 pinch cinnamon

Bring the milk to the boil and then allow to cool for 10 minutes.

Beat together egg yolks, fructose and cinnamon. Whisk until the mixture turns white and creamy.

Stir the milk and crème fraîche together and then add to the egg mixture, beating continuously.

Cover the bottom of a shallow dish or individual ramekins with raspberries and then pour the final mixture over the top.

Place the shallow dish or ramekins in a hot bain marie in a pre-heated oven (Mk. ½ – 130°C) and cook for 55 minutes.

Allow to cool to room temperature and refrigerate for at least 4 hours.

Before serving, the catalan cream can be grilled for a few minutes until golden brown.

Clafoutis aux Cerises
Cherry Flan

Serves 5   Phase 2
Preparation : 15 minutes
    Cooking : 60 minutes

- 750g (1¾lb) stoned cherries
- 20cl (7fl oz) milk
- 20cl (7fl oz) whipping cream
- 60g (2oz) fructose
- 6 eggs
- 6 tablespoons rum
- vanilla extract

Soak the cherries in the rum.

Heat the milk and the whipping cream without boiling. Allow to cool.

In a large bowl, beat together the eggs with the fructose. Pour in the milk, stirring constantly. Add a few drops of vanilla extract.

Arrange the cherries in a 28cm (11in) flan dish.

Add the rum from the cherries to the milk mixture and over the cherries in the flan.

Cook for 50 minutes in the oven (Mk. ½ – 130°C). Allow to cool before putting in the fridge. Chill completely before serving.

Châtaigner au Chocolat
Chestnut and Chocolate Mousse

Serves 5
Preparation : 20 minutes
   Cooking : 15 minutes

Phase 2

- 1.5kg (3¼lbs) chestnuts
- 200g (7oz) chocolate with 70% cocoa solids
- 100g (4oz) crème fraîche
- 3 tablespoons fructose
- 50cl (2fl oz) milk
- 1 vanilla pod (or 2cc of essence)
- 7cl (3oz) cognac

Peel the chestnuts. Boil for 5 minutes to ease removal of the inner skin.

Then cook over a low heat in the vanilla milk for about 30 minutes, until soft.

Drain and reduce to a purée using the potato masher.

Melt the chocolate with the cognac in a bain-marie.

In a large bowl, mix the chestnuts, melted chocolate, crème fraîche and fructose together thoroughly.

Line a mould with aluminium foil which has been lightly greased. Pour in the mixture. Cover with plastic film and put in the fridge for at least 5 hours.

Unmould and serve onto a melted chocolate base coating individual plates. If preferred, decorate also with whipped cream.

Truffes au Chocolat
Chocolate Truffles

This recipe makes about 30 truffles.   Phase 2

Preparation : 20 minutes
No cooking

- 160g (6oz) unsweetened cocoa powder
- 75g (3oz) fine fructose powder
- 150g (5oz) butter – unsalted
- 2 egg yolks
- 80g (3oz) crème fraîche

Remove the butter from the fridge 4 hours before starting the recipe. Do this to ensure the butter is at room temperature when you start working.

Put the butter in a basin and work with a wooden spoon until the texture is completely smooth.

Incorporate first the egg yolks, then the fructose and then the cocoa. Continue stirring with a spoon until the mixture is completely mixed and smooth again.

Add the crème fraîche and continue mixing into a stiff paste. If the mixture is too soft, return to the fridge for an hour to stiffen.

With a spoon form small balls out of the paste and then roll them in cocoa powder. Shape the truffles according to fancy.

Store in the fridge. Allow 15 minutes before serving, once the truffles have been removed from the fridge.

Flan à la Noix de Coco
Coconut Flan

Serves 4   Phase 2
Preparation : 10 minutes
    Cooking : 50 minutes

- 5 eggs
- 100g (3½oz) grated coconut
- 100g (3½oz) fructose
- 40cl (14fl oz) whipping cream

In a bowl, beat the eggs together with the fructose. Add the whipping cream. Then add the coconut.

Pour into a 1 litre (2 pint) cake tin, cover with a cloth and allow to rest for 15 minutes.

Cook for 50 to 60 minutes in a bain-marie in the oven (Mk. ½ – 130°C). Check that the flan is set (insert a skewer into the middle and it should come out clean).

Remove from the oven and allow to cool to room temperature (or until cold) before serving with a raspberry coulis or hot chocolate sauce.

Crème Caramel au Fructose
Cream Caramel with Fructose

Serves 6   Phase 2
Preparation : 15 minutes
    Cooking : 55 minutes

- 1 litre (1¾ pints) full cream milk
- 6 eggs
- 1 vanilla pod
- 150g (5oz) fructose
- 1 tablespoon cognac

Bring the milk and split vanilla pod slowly to the boil. Allow to cool.

In a mould, heat 50g (2oz) of fructose with a little water to make a caramel.

In a bowl, beat the eggs with the remaining 100g of fructose. Add the lukewarm milk little by little, beating all the time with the whisk. Add the cognac.

Pour the mixture into the mould and cook for 45 minutes in a fairly hot oven (Mk.6 – 200°C) in a bain marie. Allow to cool and then refrigerate for at least 4 hours.

To turn out, place the mould for a few seconds in boiling water. Cover with a plate and turn over quickly. Alternatively, make and serve in individual ramekins.

Crème d'Orange
Cream of Orange

Serves 4
Preparation : 20 minutes
   Cooking : 45 minutes

Phase 2

- 9 egg yolks + 1 whole egg
- 150g (5oz) fructose
- 4 or 5 oranges – to give about 30cl (10fl oz) juice
- 20cl (7fl oz) whipping cream
- zest of 1 orange

Beat together the eggs and the fructose in a large bowl.

Whisk the cream until stiff. Fold into the egg mixture.

Bring the orange juice and zest to the boil and continue boiling for 3 minutes.

Allow to cool for 5 minutes and then pour slowly into the egg mixture, stirring constantly with the whisk.

Pour the mixture into moulds and cook in a bain-marie in a pre-heated oven (Mk.½ – 130°C) for 40 minutes.

Allow to cool and refrigerate for at least 4 to 5 hours before serving.

Mousse aux Amandes Fraîches
Fresh Almond Mousse

Serves 4/5
Preparation : 25 minutes
   Cooking : 15 minutes

Phase 2

- 4 eggs
- 100g (3½oz) freshly peeled almonds
- 35cl (12fl oz) very cold whipping cream
- 100g (3½oz) red currants
- 100g (3½oz) fructose powder
- juice of ½ lemon
- 1 teaspoon lemon zest
- 1 tablespoon liquid fructose
- mint leaves to decorate

Break the eggs into a bowl and whisk with the fructose in a bain-marie over a low heat. Continue beating till the mixture becomes firm and frothy.

Remove from the bain-marie and continue whisking until the mixture has cooled. Add the lemon juice, the liquid fructose and then the lemon zest. When fully mixed, place on one side and reserve.

Wash the red currants, remove the stalks and dry on kitchen paper.

Chop the almonds. Over a low heat, lightly brown in a dry non-stick pan.

Whisk the cream until stiff. Fold in the egg mixture and and then carefully add the red currants and chopped almonds.

Line the inside of a fluted mould with plastic film. Pour in the mixture and wrap the film over the top.

Place in the fridge for 4 hours.

Unmould onto a plate. Decorate with mint leaves and serve.

Gâteau au Chocolat Fondant
Gateau with Fondant Chocolate

This dish can be served with whipped cream, vanilla ice cream or with a crème anglaise made with fructose.

Phase 2

Serves 4 to 6
Preparation : 25 minutes
   Cooking : 30 minutes

- 250g (9oz) chocolate – containing 70% cocoa solids
- 5 eggs
- 1 teaspoon orange zest
- 1 pinch salt
- 2 tablespoons cognac

Break the eggs and separate the yolks from the whites. Beat the whites with a pinch of salt until stiff.

Melt the chocolate with ½ glass of water in a bain-marie.

Take the pan out of the bain-marie, add the cognac and half the zest of orange. Stir well with a wooden spoon to obtain a very smooth mixture.

Allow to cool for 2 to 3 minutes, then add the egg yolks and mix thoroughly. Fold in the beaten whites until thoroughly mixed. Pour into a greased (20cm or 8in) cake tin which will allow the mixture to settle to a depth of 5cm (2in).

Sprinkle the remaining zest of orange over the top.

Cook for 20 minutes in a pre-heated oven (Mk.¼ – 100°C) till the cake is set and a skewer inserted into the centre comes out clean.

Gratinée de Nectarines
Grilled Nectarines and Zabaglione

Serves 4   Phase 2
Preparation: 15 minutes
    Cooking : 20 minutes

- 6 good-sized nectarines
- 5 egg yolks
- 100g (3½oz) fructose
- 20cl (7fl oz) sparkling white wine
  (Monbazillac, Sainte-Croix-du-Mont . . .)

Bring 75cl of water to the boil. Add the nectarines and poach for 5 minutes.

Drain and split the nectarines in two, to remove the stones. Then remove the skin and cut each fruit into a total of 8 sections.

Put the egg yolks and the fructose into a large bowl and whisk for 3 or 4 minutes, until they are white and creamy.

To prepare the sabayon, place the bowl with the egg mixture in a bain-marie over a low heat and continue to whisk until the mixture thickens while adding a little wine at regular intervals.

Arrange the nectarines in ovenware dishes. Pour the sabayon over the top and place under the grill for several minutes before serving.

Gratinée de Poires
Grilled Pear Zabaglione

The dishes can be covered with plastic film and stored in the
fridge, to be eaten cold or grilled very rapidly just before serving.

Phase 2

Serves 4
Preparation : 20 minutes
   Cooking : 35 minutes

- 8 nice pears
- 100g (3½oz) fructose
- 5 egg yolks
- juice of 1 orange
- 1 teaspoon vanilla extract
- 1 tablespoon rum
- mint leaves

Peel the pears, quarter and remove the cores. Slice each quarter into two.

Arrange the pear slices on the bottom of an ovenware dish lightly brushed with oil.
Sprinkle 25g (1oz) fructose over the top. Place under the grill for 5 to 10 minutes,
to allow the pears to brown lightly without burning. Reserve.

To make the sabayon, whisk the egg yolks and fructose together until they begin to turn
slightly white and creamy. Add the orange juice, vanilla, rum and cooking juice from
the pears.

Cook gently in a bain-marie, beating constantly, until the cream thickens slightly.

Arrange the pear slices on serving plates. Pour the cream over the top and decorate with
a mint leaf.

Citronnier
Lemon Mousse

Serves 4   Phase 2
Preparation : 20 minutes
    Cooking : 20 minutes

- 3 lemons
- 5 egg yolks + 1 whole egg
- 20cl (7fl oz) milk
- 20cl (7fl oz) whipping cream
- 150g (5oz) fructose
- 3 leaves gelatine (or equivalent of agar-agar)

Grate the lemon zest.

Beat the eggs with the fructose, juice of 3 lemons and the zest.

Heat the milk and allow to cool for a few minutes.

Gently pour the milk on the egg and lemon mixture, beating vigorously with a whisk.

Return to a very low heat (preferably a bain-marie) and allow the mixture to thicken while stirring constantly with the whisk. Allow to cool for 10 minutes.

Soak the leaves of gelatine in cold water for a few minutes. Squeeze dry and add to the mixture, stirring in well with the whisk. Allow to cool for 30 minutes.

Whisk the cream and fold into the mixture. Pour into ramekins brushed with egg white. Cover with plastic film and refrigerate for 5 to 6 hours before serving.

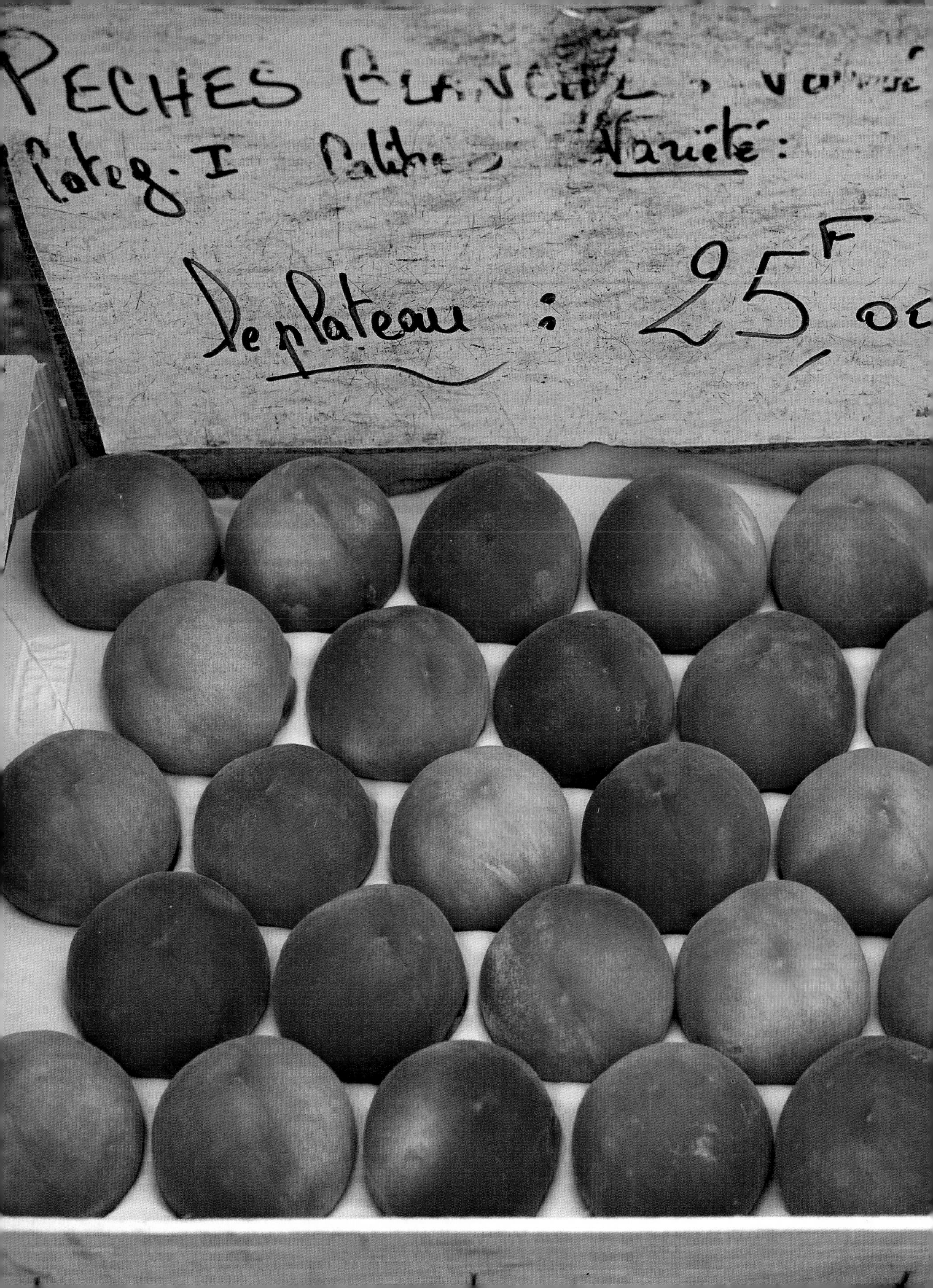
PECHES
Categ. I
Variété :
le plateau : 25F

Pêches au Fromage et aux Framboises
Peaches with Cheese and Raspberries

Serves 4
Preparation : 10 minutes
   Cooking : 10 minutes

Phase 2

- 500g (18oz) fromage frais – strained
- 2 tablespoons crème fraîche
- 6 nice peaches
- 100g (3½oz) sugar-free raspberry jam
- mint leaves

Poach the peaches for about 10 minutes. Peel, halve and remove the stones.

Liquidize the fromage frais, crème fraîche and raspberry jam. Pour into the bottom of individual dipped plates. Arrange 3 peach halves on top of each plate. Cover with plastic film and place in the fridge:

Serve chilled and decorate with mint.

Poires au Vin
Pears in Wine

Serves 4
Preparation : 20 minutes
   Cooking : 20 minutes

Phase 2

- 4 to 6 pears according to size
- 25cl (8fl oz) red wine with a high tannin content,
  like Corbières, Bordeaux, Côtes du Rhône . . .
- 3 tablespoons fructose
- cinnamon, nutmeg
- pepper, pimento (sweet pepper)

Peel the pears and keep the stalk. Place them in a pan, just large enough for them to fit snugly. Add the wine and fructose.

Bring to the boil and cook for 10 minutes with the lid covering about two-thirds of the pan, to ensure the wine does not boil over.

Remove from the heat and turn the pears.

Add 2 or 3 pinches of cinnamon, sweet paprika, grated nutmeg and freshly ground pepper.

Return to the heat as before and cook for a further 10 minutes.

Check the pears are properly cooked by testing with the sharp point of a knife, and reserve on a separate dish.

Reduce the wine syrup in the casserole to thicken, stirring constantly to avoid it catching on the bottom of the pan.

Arrange the pears in bowls and coat with the syrup.

Bavarois de Framboise et son Coulis
Raspberry Bavarois with its Coulis

Serves 4   Phase 2
Preparation : 20 minutes
  Cooking : 5 minutes

- 750g (1½lb) raspberries
- 1 lemon
- 3 tablespoons fructose
- 150g (5oz) fromage frais
- 15cl (5fl oz) whipping cream
- 5 leaves of gelatine (or the equivalent of agar-agar)

Liquidize the the raspberries and put through a conical sieve to remove the pips if necessary.

Drain the fromage frais.

Add the lemon juice and fructose.

Reserve a third of the mixture in the fridge, for making the coulis later.

Using a bain-marie, dissolve the gelatine leaves in 2 tablespoons of water and immediately add the two-thirds of the raspberry purée. Mix in with the drained fromage frais and the whipping cream.

Pour into small moulds brushed with egg white and place in the fridge for 6 hours or until the mixture begins to set.

Turn out the moulds onto individual plates and surround the bavarois with the coulis. Decorate with a mint leaf and serve.

Framboisier
Raspberry Bush

Serves 4/5   Phase 2
Preparation : 20 minutes
    Cooking : 20 minutes

- 250g (8oz) raspberries
- 4 egg yolks
- ½ litre (18fl oz) full cream milk
- 2 tablespoons fructose
- 1 vanilla pod
- 4 leaves gelatine (or equivalent of agar-agar)
- 20cl (7fl oz) whipping cream

Split the vanilla pod and add to the milk. Bring the milk slowly to the boil and allow to cool for 10 minutes.

Beat the egg yolks and pour in the milk gradually while continuing to whisk.

Return the mixture to a pan over a very low heat (preferably a bain-marie) and allow to thicken slightly. Stir constantly with a whisk. Add the fructose.

Soak the leaves of gelatine in cold water for a few minutes. Squeeze out and add to the egg mixture, mixing in well with the whisk so that the gelatine dissolves completely. Place on one side and allow to cool for 1 hour.

Whip the cream and fold into the egg mixture before it sets.

Pour the mixture into moulds together with the raspberries.

Cover with plastic film and place in the fridge for at least 5 or 6 hours.

Serve plain or with whipped cream, sprinkled with cocoa or grated chocolate.

Fruits Rouges en Gelée de Vin Rouge
Red Fruit in Red Wine Jelly

Serves 6   Phase 2
Preparation : 20 minutes
    Cooking : 10 minutes

- 200g (7oz) strawberries
- 200g (7oz) raspberries
- 100g (3½oz) blueberries
- 100g (3½oz) blackberries
- 40cl (14fl oz) red wine with a high tannin content,
  like Corbières, Côtes du Rhône . . .
- 10cl (3½fl oz) liquid fructose (or 4 tablespoons)
- ½ teaspoon cinnamon
- 7 leaves gelatine (or the equivalent of agar-agar)
- mint leaves

Place a fluted mould in the freezer.

Pour the wine into a pan and add the cinnamon. Bring to the boil and remove immediately from the heat.

Meanwhile, prepare the fruit.

Soften the gelatine for 5 minutes in cold water. Squeeze out and then dissolve in the warm wine. Add the liquid fructose. Stir well and allow to cool.

Take the mould out of the freezer and coat the inside with the wine jelly by tipping the mould from side to side, making sure no part is left uncovered by the jelly.

Return the mould to the freezer for a few minutes and repeat the coating operation until the jelly lining is about 1cm thick (just under ½in) all over.

Turn the fruit into the mould. Spread out well using a spoon or spatula and layer of mint leaves.

Pour the rest of the wine jelly carefully over the top and cover with aluminium foil.

Leave in the fridge overnight or for at least 8 or 10 hours.

Unmould just prior to serving.

Gâteau aux Pommes Paysan
Rustic Apple Cake

Serves 5
Preparation : 25 minutes
   Cooking : 20 minutes

Phase 2

- 6 or 7 apples
- 150g (5oz) fructose
- 10 eggs + 2 yolks
- 20cl (7fl oz) whipping cream
- fructose glaze

Quarter, peel, core and slice the apples (about 4 slices per quarter).

Grease a large non-stick pan (25cm or 8in in diameter) with a paper kitchen towel soaked in oil.

Arrange the apple slices on the bottom of the pan.

Break the eggs into a bowl. Add the yolks, cream and half the fructose. Beat together.

Sprinkle the apples with the rest of the fructose and cook gently until they have lost some of their moisture and are tender.

When the apples are soft and slightly transparent, add the egg mixture and continue to cook.

When two-thirds of the omelette has cooked, put the pan under the grill to complete the cooking and make the top golden-brown.

Sprinkle the top with the fructose glaze and serve.

Fraises à la Menthe et au Yaourt
Strawberries with Mint and Yoghurt

Serves 4   Phase 2
Preparation : 15 minutes
No cooking

- 750g (1½lb) strawberries
- 3 cartons yoghurt
- 1 large bunch of mint
- 2 tablespoons of sugar-free strawberry jam

Rinse, drain on kitchen paper and remove the stalks from the strawberries. Arrange in small bowls.

Remove the mint leaves from their stems and chop finely.

In a bowl, mix the yoghurt, chopped mint and strawberry jam. Chill in the fridge.

Pour over the strawberries and serve.

Fraises à l'Orange Mentholée
Strawberries with Orange and Mint

Serves 4   Phase 2
Preparation : 10 minutes
     Cooking : 15 minutes

- 500g (1lb) strawberries
- 3 oranges
- ½ glass cointreau
- 50g fructose
- 12 leaves of mint

Squeeze the juice out of the oranges.

Put the orange juice, cointreau, fructose and 5 chopped mint leaves into a small pan. Bring to the boil and reduce by half. Allow to cool.

Rinse the strawberries under the tap and drain on kitchen paper.

Remove the stalks and cut in two.

Arrange in individual plates.

Coat with the minted syrup of orange.

Decorate with the remaining mint leaves and serve.

MENUS

for three months

(Weight Reduction Programme)

General Comments

These menus have been prepared for those who want to use the recipes in this book to lose weight and would like to know how to structure their meals over an extended period to achieve their goal.

All the dishes in the menu programme conform to Phase 1 – the weight reduction phase of the Montignac Method – though the rules have been slightly relaxed for lunch on Saturdays and Sundays. Those not prepared to lose weight in a leisurely fashion, should skip the desserts.

Some may be surprised to find cooked apples featuring in some of the recipes. Although they have never been excluded from Phase 1, the recommendation that raw fruit should only be eaten on an empty stomach has led some people to eliminate cooked fruit from their meals altogether.

This is to misunderstand the reason for recommending that raw fruit should be eaten on an empty stomach. The reason is quite simple: with the exception of red fruit like strawberries and raspberries, raw fruit eaten at the end of a meal or after other foods, is liable to ferment in the stomach and upset the digestive process. The advice that raw fruit should be eaten on an empty stomach and at least 20 minutes before eating other foods, has been given for reasons of personal comfort – not because eating fruit promotes weight gain.

It is important to realise that when fruit is cooked, the risk that it will ferment in the stomach is virtually non-existent. That is why certain fruits with a low glycaemic index, like apples, can be included in the programme without any problems.

I would conclude by reminding everybody following the Montignac Method, that a balanced diet requires an adequate intake of good carbohydrates at breakfast time – namely, wholemeal bread (or better still, bread made with unrefined flour), sugar-free jam or cereals like muesli (without added sugar). Fresh fruit is also essential, but it must be eaten on an empty stomach and at least 20 minutes before eating anything else.

FIRST MONTH – Week 1

Lunch			Dinner	
Lambs Ear Salad Chicken Breast with Lime French Beans Cheese	144	**M**	Smooth Mushroom Soup Tomatoes Stuffed with Cracked Wheat Yoghurt	80 60
Tomato Salad Veal Escalope with Parma Cream Peas Cheese	134	**T**	Cheese Soufflé Green Salad Yoghurt	42
Mushroom Salad Mackerel in White Wine Chicory Cheese	277	**W**	Cauliflower Salad Fried Eggs and Cured Ham Fromage Frais	87
Celery with Mayonnaise Trout with Almonds Spinach Purée Cheese	211	**T**	Cream of Leek Soup Montignac Spaghetti with Tomato Sauce Fat-free Yoghurt	69
Aubergine Marinade Turkey Pot-au-feu Cheese	34 180	**F**	Sorrel Soup Broccoli Salad with Almonds Yoghurt	81 271
Beef Carpaccio Roast Pork with Curry Brussel Sprouts from Gers Cheese Apple Scramble with Cinnamon	39 124 241 286	**S**	Tomato Consommé Monkfish American Style Cheese	82 196
Avocado Paté with Prawns Salmon in a Salt Crust Steamed Broccoli Chestnut and Chocolate Mousse	38 203 297	**S**	Scrambled Eggs with Red Peppers Salad Cheese	93

FIRST MONTH – Week 2

Lunch				Dinner	
Chicory Salad		**M**		Farmhouse Quiche	248
Pork Shoulder Provençale	120			Salad	
Ratatouille	254			Full Fat Yoghurt	
Cheese					
Bean Shoot Salad		**T**		Cucumber with Low-fat Yoghurt	
Calfs Liver with Onions	109			Whole-grain rice with Tomato Coulis	
Cheese				Stewed Apples	
Chilled Cucumber Soup		**W**		Mussels with Soya Cream	224
Grilled Salmon with Tamari Sauce	190			Green Salad	
Broccoli				Full-fat Yoghurt	
Cheese					
Sweet Peppers Polka with Bacon	59	**T**		Montignac Tagliatelle with Pesto	259
Beef Casserole Provençale	105			Low-fat Fromage Frais	
Celeriac Purée	245				
Yoghurt					
Avocado		**F**		Tortilla Montignac	98
Chicken Breasts Provençale	145			Green Salad	
Green Salad				Full-fat Yoghurt	
Cheese					
Cheese and Onion Rösti	40	**S**		Cream of Leek Soup	69
Cod Provençale	184			Squid Provençale	208
Braised Leeks	239			Cream Caramel	302
Cheese					
Monkfish Terrine	53	**S**		Scrambled Eggs with Sorrel	94
Scallops with Shallots	228			Green Salad	
Improvised Salad				Cheese	
Apricot Bavarois	288				

FIRST MONTH – Week 3

Lunch			Dinner	
Mussel Salad Chicken Breasts and Tarragon in a Bag Steamed Chicory Cheese	142	M	Leek Clafoutis Green Salad Baked Apples	250
Chicory Salad Veal with Paprika Cheese	135	T	Montignac Spaghetti with Tomato Coulis Fat-free Yoghurt	
Leek Vinaigrette Grilled Tuna Steak Ratatouille Cheese	254	W	Fish soup Ramekin Eggs with Tarragon Salad with Warm Goats Cheese	91
Smooth Mushroom Soup Entrecote Steaks Bordeaux Style French Beans Cheese	80 111	T	Grated Carrots with Lemon Juice Lentils in Tomato Sauce Low-fat Fromage Frais	
Chicken Salad Scrambled Eggs with Red Peppers Cheese	273 93	F	Cured Ham with Courgettes and Parmesan Green Salad Soya Yoghurt	247
Celeriac and Avocado Remoulade Rolled Escalopes with Ham Provençale Style Salad Raspberry Bush	272 127 315	S	Chicken Provençale Green Salad Yoghurt	151
Oysters Pigeon with Thyme Stuffing Celeriac Purée Gateau with Fondant Chocolate	173 245 306	S	Cream of Garlic Soup Poached Eggs Provençale Salad Cheese	68 89

FIRST MONTH – Week 4

Lunch			Dinner	
Radishes		**M**	Vegetable Soup	
Tuna, Tomato and Scrambled Egg	214		Chicken Liver Terrine	43
Chicory Salad			Salad	
Cheese			Fromage Frais	
Palm Hearts		**T**	Smooth Broccoli Soup	
Veal Escalopes with Parma Cream	134		Wholegrain rice and Tomato Coulis	
Cauliflower Purée			Low Fat Yoghurt	
Cheese				
Mushroom Salad	277	**W**	Cabbage Soup	66
Onion Gratinée	251		Courgette and Sweet Pepper Flan	45
Yoghurt			Cheese	
Red Cabbage Salad with Walnuts	280	**T**	Grated Carrots with Lemon Juice	
Goujons of Veal	114		Wholemeal pasta with Tomato	
Braised Chicory	236		and Basil Coulis	
Cheese			Low-fat Yoghurt	
Avocado Vinaigrette		**F**	Mushroom Omelette	
Pork Chops with Cream of Mustard Sauce	119		Salad	
Braised Chicory	236		Yoghurt	
Cheese				
Marinated Salmon		**S**	Cream of Mussel Soup	70
Blanquette of Veal Montignac	106		Sea Bream Basque Style	207
Peaches with Cheese and Raspberries	311		Braised Leeks	239
			Cheese	
Sorrel Soup	81	**S**	Tomato Flan	260
Roast Breast of Duck	175		Salad	
Parsley Mushrooms	253		Baked Apples	
Fresh Almond Mousse	304			

SECOND MONTH – Week 1

Lunch			Dinner	
Cauliflower Vinaigrette		**M**	Tomato Consommé	82
Chicken with Garlic	155		Skewered Vegetables Provençale	256
Celeriac Purée	245		Low-fat Yoghurt	
Cheese				
Aubergine Marinade	34	**T**	Cretan Style Feta Terrine	46
Roast Pork with Curry	124		Cheese Omelette	
Brussel Sprouts			Green Salad	
Cheese			Yoghurt	
Tomato and Feta Cheese Salad		**W**	Tomatoes Stuffed with Cracked Wheat	60
Lemon Sole Cretan Style	195		Salad	
Spinach			Baked Apples	
Cheese				
Red Cabbage Salad with Walnuts	280	**T**	Cabbage Soup	66
Steak Tartare			Montignac Spaghetti with	
Cheese			Tomato and Courgette Sauce	
			Low-fat Yoghurt	
Chicory Salad with Walnuts		**F**	Tuna with Garlic Vinegar	216
Rack of Lamb Provençale	122		Aubergine Gratin	234
Parsley Mushrooms	253		Cheese	
Yoghurt				
Watercress and Bacon Salad	283	**S**	Green Salad with Pine Nuts	
Grilled Sea Bass with Fennel and Pastis	192		Poached Eggs Provençale	89
Braised Leeks	239		Yoghurt	
Lemon Mousse	309			
Giant Scampi and Mayonnaise		**S**	Cream of Watercress Soup	
Duck Breasts with Orange	163		Artichokes Vinaigrette	
Tomato Salad			Cheese	
Raspberry Bush	315			

SECOND MONTH – Week 2

Lunch			Dinner	
Mushroom Salad	277	**M**	Tomato Consommé	82
Beef Casserole Provençale	105		Green Salad	
Celeriac Purée	245		Low-fat Yoghurt	
Cheese				
Palm Hearts		**T**	Cheese Soufflé	42
Roast Pork			Green Salad	
Grilled Aubergines			Baked Apples	
Cheese				
Marinated Goats Cheese	50	**W**	Cream of Soya with Shallots	73
with Fresh Broad Beans			Chicken Breasts Provençale	145
Grilled Giant Prawns			Salad	
Spinach with Soya Cream	257		Yoghurt	
Feta Cheese				
Tuna Tartare	213	**T**	Grated Carrots with Lemon Juice	
Duck Breasts with Olives	161		Tagliatelle with Pesto	259
Salad			Low-fat Yoghurt	
Cheese				
Radishes		**F**	Mimosa Eggs with Tuna	88
Turkey Escalopes with Cream	179		Salad with Warm Goats Cheese	
Braised Courgettes				
Cheese				
Provençale Cheese Mousse	54	**S**	Cream of Shrimp Soup	72
Fillets of Sole with Salmon	186		Sea Bass with Shallot Sauce	204
Broccoli			Spinach and Soya Cream	257
Brazilian Mousse	292		Yoghurt	
Scallops and Grated Cheese	58	**S**	French Onion Soup	
Turkey Pot-au-Feu	180		Skewered Vegetables Provençale	256
Catalan Cream	293		Cheese	
			Green Salad	
			White Cheese with Herbs	

SECOND MONTH – Week 3

Lunch			Dinner	
Broccoli Salad with Almonds	271	**M**	Vegetable Broth	
Pork Chops with Mustard Sauce	119		Tomatoes Stuffed with Cracked Wheat	60
Cheese			Low-fat Yoghurt	
Cucumber and Tomato Salad	39	**T**	Provençale Cheese Mousse	54
Green Salad			Chicken Kebab	
Cheese			Salad	
			Yoghurt	
French Bean Vinaigrette		**W**	Leek Broth	
Filets of Sole with Cream of Soya Sauce	185		Red Bean Salad	278
Cheese			Low-fat Yoghurt with Sugar-free Jam	
Bacon and Broadbean Salad	269	**T**	Cream of Leek Soup	69
Grilled Duck's Breast			Chicken Liver Terrine	44
Salsify			Fromage Frais en Faiselle	
Cheese				
Prawn Avocado	184	**F**	Tomato Consommé	82
Steamed Leek Vinaigrette			Montignac Spaghetti	
Cheese			with Tomato and Basil	
			Low-fat Yoghurt	
Watercress and Bacon Salad	285	**S**	Squid Provençale	208
Fish Soup with Shellfish	188		Rustic Apple Cake	318
Catalan Cream	293			
Aumonière of Smoked Salmon Mousse	35	**S**	Smooth Mushroom Soup	80
Red Mullet with Cream Sauce	202		Scrambled Eggs with Sorrel	94
French Bean Purée				
Apple Soufflé Flambé	287			

SECOND MONTH – Week 4

Lunch			Dinner	
Cucumber Salad Turkey with Apples Fromage Frais en Faiselle	181	**M**	Asparagus Soup Haricot Beans with Tomato Coulis Fat-free Yoghurt with Sugar-free Jam	
Chicory Salad with Walnuts Grilled Salmon Steak French Beans Cheese		**T**	Sorrel Soup Chicken Liver and Leek Terrine Green Salad Yoghurt	81 44
Cheese and Onion Rösti Tuna, Tomato and Scrambled Eggs Cheese	40 214	**W**	Chilled Cream of Cucumber Soup Farmhouse Quiche Green Salad	67 248
Celeriac and Avocado Remoulade Mutton Fillet Provençale Ratatouille Cheese	272 118 254	**T**	Fish Soup Trout with Almonds Salad Fromage Frais en Faiselle	211
Salade Niçoise Duck Breast with Olives Tomato salad Cheese	161	**F**	Tomato Consommé Wholemeal Pasta with Red Pepper Purée White Cheese with Herbs	82
Smoked Salmon Roast Beef French Beans Pears Belle-Helène		**S**	Cream of Soya and Shallots Artichokes Provençale Yoghurt	73 233
Scallops Marinated with Dill Red Mullet with Cream Sauce Steamed Broccoli Vinaigrette Fresh Almond Mousse	55 202 304	**S**	Fried Eggs and Cured Ham Green Salad Yoghurt	87

THIRD MONTH – Week 1

Lunch			Dinner	
Cauliflower Salad		**M**	Asparagus Broth	
Chicken with Garlic	155		Couscous with Red Peppers	
Braised Fennel	237		Low-fat Yoghurt	
Cheese				
Watercress and Bacon Salad	283	**T**	Cream of Garlic Soup	68
Grilled Black Pudding			Chicken Breast Tarragon	142
Apple Purée			Green Salad	
Cheese			Fromage Frais en Faiselle	
Tomato Salad with Feta Cheese		**W**	Tortilla Montignac	98
Fillets of Sole			Green Salad	
Aubergine Purée			Yoghurt	
Fromage Frais en Faiselle				
Red Cabbage Salad	280	**T**	Tomato Consommé	82
Veal with Paprika	135		Montignac Tagliatelle with	
Celeriac Purée	245		Mushroom Purée	
Cheese			Fat-free Yoghurt	
Avocado Bavarois	37	**F**	Sauerkraut Soup	78
Swordfish on Skewers	210		Goujons of Veal	114
Ratatouille	254		Braised Chicory	236
Cheese			Baked Apples	
Aumonière with Smoked Salmon Mousse	35	**S**	Fish Soup	
Leg of Lamb with Rosemary	117		Squid Provençale	208
French Beans			Salad	
Grilled Nectarines and Zabaglione	307			
Cheese				
Courgette and Sweet Pepper Flan	45	**S**	Scrambled Eggs with Prawns	92
Tournedos Provençale	129		Salad	
Parsley Mushrooms	253		Cheese	
Cream Caramel	302			

THIRD MONTH – Week 2

Lunch			Dinner	
Bacon and Broadbean Salad	269	**M**	Grated Carrots with Lemon Juice	
Partridge with Cabbage	169		Lentils with Tomato Coulis	
Cheese			Fat-free Yoghurt	
Bean Sprout Salad		**T**	Cheese Omelette	
Calfs Liver with Basil	108		Salad	
Braised Chicory	236		Yoghurt	
Cheese				
Tomato and Mozzarella Salad		**W**	Pistou Soup	76
Fresh Sardines with Sherry Vinegar	49		Fromage Frais en Faiselle	
Steamed Broccoli				
Cheese				
French Bean Salad		**T**	Tomatoes Stuffed with Cracked Wheat	60
Entrecote Steaks Bordeaux Style	111		Fat-free Yoghurt	
Red Pepper Purée				
Cheese				
Cucumber Salad		**F**	Aubergine Marinade	34
Duck with Olives	164		Fried Eggs and Cured Ham	87
Tomato Flan	260		Cheese	
Cheese				
Scallop Timbales	56	**S**	Andalousian Gaspacho	64
English Leg of Lamb	110		Turbot with Sorrel	219
Broccoli			Salad	
Brazilian Mousse	292		Apricots and Custard	290
Provençale Cheese Mousse	54	**S**	Scrambled Eggs with Sorrel	94
Turbot with Fennel	218		Salad	
Green Salad			Yoghurt	
Cherry Flan	294			

THIRD MONTH – Week 3

Lunch				Dinner	
Palm Hearts Turkey Escalopes with Cream Cheese	179	**M**		Cream of Leek Soup Stuffed Courgettes with White Cheese Yoghurt	69
Fresh Spinach Salad Pepper Steak French Bean Purée Cheese		**T**		Avocado Chicken Provençale Salad Yoghurt	151
Steamed Leeks Vinaigrette Trout with Almonds Spinach Purée Cheese	211	**W**		Pesto Soup Couscous with Red Pepper Salad Salad Fat-free Fromage Frais with Herbs	76
Red Cabbage Vinaigrette Skewered Vegetables Provençale Cheese	256	**T**		Dandelion Soup Lemon Sole Cretan Style Braised Fennel Yoghurt	75 194 237
Parsley Mushrooms Chicken Livers French Beans Cheese	253	**F**		Andalousian Gaspacho Soup Red Kidney Beans and Artichoke Hearts and Fat-free Fromage Frais	64
Asparagus Chicken Casserole in Wine Celeriac Purée Pears in Wine Cheese	146 245 312	**S**		Onion Gratinée Ramekin Eggs with Tarragon Salad	251 91
Scallops Marinated with Dill Flambé of Guinea Fowl Blanc-mange with Raspberry Coulis	55 167 291	**S**		Montignac Tortils Pasta with Tomato and Basil Sauce Fat-free Yoghurt	

THIRD MONTH – Week 4

Lunch				Dinner	
Green Salad with Warm Goat's Cheese		**M**		Chilled Cream of Cucumber Soup	67
Pork Chops with Cream of Mustard Sauce	119			Artichoke Provençale	233
Braised Fennel	237			Yoghurt	
Cheese					
Palm Hearts		**T**		Leek Clafoutis	250
Duck Breast Casserole	158			Green Salad	
Traditional Cabbage	261			Fromage Frais en Faiselle	
Cheese					
Radishes		**W**		Beef Carpaccio	39
Normandy Sole	197			Tomatoes Stuffed with Cracked Wheat	249
Cauliflower Gratin	242			Fat-free Fromage Frais with Herbs	
Cheese					
Smoked Salmon		**T**		Skewered Vegetables Provençale	256
Blanquette of Veal Montignac	106			Tuna with Garlic Vinegar	216
Cheese				Salad	
				Yoghurt	
Avocado Bavarois	37	**F**		Cream of Soya with Shallots	73
Calf's Liver with Basil	108			Tomato Flan	260
Broccoli Salad with Almonds	271			Green Salad	
Cheese				Yoghurt	
Cheese and Onion Rösti	40	**S**		Sorrel Soup	81
Chicken with Cep Mushrooms	154			Trout with Almonds	211
Raspberry Bavarois	314			Broccoli Salad	
				Cheese	
Gourmand Salad	276	**S**		Montignac Spaghetti with Tomato Sauce	
Salmon in a Salt Crust	203			Low Fat Yoghurt	
Braised Fennel	237				
Grilled Pear Zabaglione	308				